Family Law: Foundations and Modern Dynamics

Welcome to "Family Law: Foundations and Modern Dynamics," a comprehensive exploration of one of the most vital and evolving areas of law that directly impacts the lives of individuals and families. Family law is a multifaceted field that governs various aspects of familial relationships, from marriage and divorce to child custody and support, and it plays a critical role in shaping the dynamics of modern families.

This book seeks to provide a thorough understanding of the historical foundations and current complexities of family law, delving into its underlying principles, statutes, and precedents. It will take you on a journey through the evolution of family law, tracing its roots in ancient societies to its modern-day significance in shaping legal rights and responsibilities within families.

Family law has consistently adapted to reflect changing societal norms and values, making it an ever-evolving field with significant implications for individuals, communities, and society as a whole. It navigates complex issues such as parental rights, adoption, domestic violence, and same-sex unions, reflecting the diversity and dynamics of family structures today.

Throughout this book, you will explore the core principles that guide family law, such as the best interests of the child, equitable distribution, and the protection of individual rights. We will examine landmark court cases and pivotal legal decisions that have shaped the landscape of family law and influenced its development over time.

Furthermore, "Family Law: Foundations and Modern Dynamics" seeks to shed light on the challenges and controversies that have arisen in this field, as well as the ongoing efforts to promote fairness, justice, and family welfare. It aims to equip legal practitioners, students, and interested readers with the knowledge and insights necessary to navigate the intricacies of family law in today's legal system.

As we embark on this journey through the intricate realm of family law, we invite you to explore the legal principles and social dynamics that influence the ways families are recognized, protected, and supported under the law. Together, let us delve into the intricacies of this multifaceted field and gain a deeper appreciation for the profound impact it has on individuals, families, and society at large.

I. Introduction to Family Law

- Definition and scope of family law
- Historical development and societal context
- Key principles and objectives of family law

II. Marriage and Legal Partnerships

- Legal requirements for marriage
- Rights and responsibilities of spouses
- Marital agreements and prenuptial agreements
- Recognition of common-law partnerships

III. Divorce and Dissolution of Marriage

- Grounds for divorce
- Legal processes for divorce and annulment
- Division of assets and property
- Spousal support and alimony

IV. Child Custody and Support

- Types of child custody arrangements
- Determining the best interests of the child
- Child support guidelines and calculations
- Child custody modifications and enforcement

V. Adoption and Surrogacy

- Legal requirements and procedures for adoption
- Open adoption and closed adoption
- Surrogacy agreements and legal parentage
- International adoption and legal considerations

VI. LGBTQ+ Rights and Family Law

- Same-sex marriage and legal recognition
- LGBTQ+ parenting and adoption rights
- Family law challenges and advancements for LGBTQ+ couples

VII. Family Law and Reproductive Technologies

- Assisted reproductive technologies (ART)
- Legal implications of surrogacy and egg/sperm donation
- Parental rights and legal parentage in ART cases

VIII. Domestic Violence and Family Law

- Legal protections for victims of domestic violence
- Restraining orders and protective orders
- Impact of domestic violence on child custody and

visitation

IX. Family Dispute Resolution

- Mediation and alternative dispute resolution in family law
- Collaborative law and its benefits
- Litigation and court proceedings in family disputes

X. International Family Law

- Cross-border family law issues and jurisdiction
- International child abduction and the Hague Convention
- Recognition of foreign marriages and divorces

XI. Family Law and Child Welfare

- Child protection services and legal interventions
- Foster care and kinship care arrangements
- Termination of parental rights and adoption

XII. Family Law and Elder Care

- Legal issues in elder care and guardianship
- Advance directives and end-of-life decisions
- Long-term care planning and financing

XIII. Family Law and Mental Health

- Mental health considerations in family law disputes
- Involuntary commitment and legal rights
- Mental health and child custody evaluations

XIV. Family Law and Inheritance

- Intestate succession and wills
- Inheritance rights of surviving spouses and children
- Estate planning and family law considerations

XV. Future Trends and Challenges in Family Law

- Evolving family structures and legal implications
- Technological advancements and family law
- Balancing cultural diversity and legal uniformity

XVI. Conclusion

- Recapitulation of key insights and themes discussed in the book
- The importance of family law in shaping relationships and society's well-being

Definition and scope of family law

Family law is a specialized branch of law that deals with legal matters and issues relating to familial relationships and domestic affairs. It encompasses a wide range of legal issues that arise within families, including marriage, divorce, child custody and visitation, child support, adoption, domestic violence, property division, and more. Family law governs the rights, responsibilities, and obligations of family members and seeks to protect the best interests of all parties involved.

The scope of family law is extensive and continuously evolving, reflecting the changing nature of family structures and societal norms. It varies from one jurisdiction to another, as each country or state may have its own specific laws and regulations concerning family matters. Family law often involves complex legal and emotional considerations, requiring sensitivity and compassion from legal practitioners and judges.

Family law serves as a crucial tool in resolving disputes and providing legal remedies in family-related matters. Its primary focus is to safeguard the well-being of individuals and families, particularly vulnerable parties such as children and victims of domestic violence. It also aims to ensure the fair and equitable distribution of assets and resources in cases of divorce or separation.

Family law practitioners, including family lawyers and judges, play a significant role in facilitating negotiations and mediating disputes between family members to achieve amicable resolutions whenever possible. However, in cases where amicable agreements are not possible, family law courts are tasked with making decisions that are in the best interests of the involved parties.

Given the sensitive and personal nature of family law cases, legal professionals in this field often work closely with social workers, counselors, and other experts to provide comprehensive support and resources to families in need. The overarching goal of family law is to promote the well-being and stability of families while upholding the principles of justice and fairness.

In conclusion, family law is an essential and dynamic area of legal practice that addresses a wide range of issues affecting families and their members. From traditional to non-traditional family structures, it encompasses the legal framework that underpins the relationships, responsibilities, and rights within families, shaping the lives of individuals and the fabric of society.

Historical development and societal context

The roots of family law can be traced back to ancient civilizations, where the regulation of familial relationships and domestic affairs was an integral part of societal norms and religious customs. Early legal systems in civilizations such as ancient Mesopotamia, Egypt, Greece, and Rome had laws pertaining to marriage, divorce, property rights, and inheritance.

In ancient Mesopotamia, for instance, the Code of Hammurabi, one of the oldest legal codes known to humanity, included provisions related to family matters, such as marriage contracts, divorce, and the rights of children. In ancient Rome, the legal institution of marriage was a central aspect of family life, and divorce was also recognized.

Throughout history, family law has been influenced by cultural, religious, and societal norms. In medieval Europe, the Christian Church played a significant role in regulating marriage and family life. The Canon Law of the Catholic Church had a profound impact on marriage and divorce laws, and the Church's influence extended to issues of legitimacy and inheritance.

During the Renaissance and Enlightenment periods, family law began to evolve alongside broader changes in society, as new ideas about individual rights and equality emerged. The concept of the nuclear family, consisting of parents and their children, gained prominence during this time.

In the 19th and 20th centuries, family law underwent significant transformations in response to changing social values and the advancement of women's rights. The rise of feminism and the women's suffrage movement led to reforms in marriage and divorce laws, giving women greater autonomy and legal rights within the family.

Family law has continued to evolve in modern times, reflecting shifts in societal norms, family structures, and reproductive technologies. The recognition of same-sex marriages and the legal rights of LGBTQ+ families is an example of how family law has adapted to address the changing landscape of familial relationships.

Today, family law remains a dynamic and evolving field, influenced by ongoing debates surrounding topics such as surrogacy, adoption, assisted reproductive technologies, and the rights of children in diverse family configurations. The intersection of family law with issues of gender equality, children's rights, and domestic violence underscores its importance in shaping the fabric of society and promoting justice and fairness within families.

In conclusion, the historical development of family law reflects the ever-changing dynamics of familial relationships and societal values. From ancient civilizations to the modern era, family law has played a critical role in regulating family life and addressing the legal needs and rights of individuals within the family unit. Its ongoing evolution continues to be shaped by the complexities of contemporary society, making it a vital and enduring area of legal practice.

Key principles and objectives of family law

Family law encompasses a wide range of legal principles and objectives aimed at regulating familial relationships, protecting the interests of family members, and promoting the well-being of individuals within the family unit. Some of the key principles and objectives of family law include:

1. Marriage and Divorce: Family law governs the legal aspects of marriage, including the requirements for marriage, the recognition of marriages performed in different jurisdictions, and the procedures for obtaining a divorce or annulment.

2. Child Custody and Support: Family law addresses matters related to child custody, visitation rights, and child support. The primary concern is the best interests of the child, ensuring their well-being and proper care.

3. Property and Financial Rights: Family law deals with the division of property and assets during divorce or separation. It aims to achieve equitable distribution of marital property and financial resources, taking into account the contributions of each spouse to the marriage.

4. Domestic Violence and Protection Orders: One of the crucial objectives of family law is to protect individuals from domestic violence and abuse. It provides for the issuance of protection orders to safeguard victims and prevent further harm.

5. Adoption and Surrogacy: Family law governs the legal processes for adoption and surrogacy, ensuring

the legal recognition of parental rights and responsibilities in these unique family formations.

6. Parental Rights and Responsibilities: Family law establishes the rights and responsibilities of parents towards their children, including decision-making authority, financial support, and parenting time.

7. Paternity and Parentage: Family law addresses the determination of paternity and parentage, ensuring that children have legal rights and support from both biological parents.

8. Mediation and Dispute Resolution: Family law encourages alternative dispute resolution methods, such as mediation, to promote amicable resolutions in family matters, reducing the emotional and financial toll of litigation.

9. International Family Law: With the globalization of families, family law addresses issues related to international child abduction, cross-border marriages, and the recognition of foreign judgments.

10. Protection of Vulnerable Family Members: Family law includes provisions to protect vulnerable family members, such as minors, elderly individuals, and individuals with disabilities, ensuring their rights and interests are safeguarded.

11. Foster Care and Child Welfare: Family law oversees the legal framework for foster care, child protection, and the intervention of child welfare agencies when necessary to ensure a child's safety and well-being.

12. Family Dispute Resolution: Encouraging the resolution of family disputes through non-adversarial means, family law seeks to minimize conflicts and promote healthier family relationships.

Overall, the fundamental principles and objectives of family law revolve around preserving the integrity of the family unit, ensuring the protection of individual rights, and promoting the best interests of family members, especially children. The application of these principles may vary across jurisdictions, but they form the core framework for addressing the complex legal issues that arise within the context of family life.

Marriage and Legal Partnerships

Marriage and legal partnerships are central components of family law, governing the legal recognition of relationships between individuals and their rights and obligations towards each other. Let's explore each of them in more detail:

1. Marriage: Marriage is a formal union between two individuals that is recognized by law. It creates a legal and social relationship between spouses, entailing specific rights and responsibilities. Family law governs the legal requirements for marriage, including age restrictions, consent, and capacity to marry. It also defines the legal consequences of marriage, such as property rights, inheritance, and spousal support.

2. Civil Partnerships and Domestic Partnerships: In some jurisdictions, civil partnerships or domestic partnerships are recognized as legal unions similar to marriage. These partnerships may provide some or all of the legal rights and benefits of marriage without the formal religious or cultural aspects.

3. Common-Law Marriage: In certain regions, common-law marriage is recognized, where a couple is considered legally married after living together for a specific period and meeting certain requirements. Family law addresses the legal recognition and dissolution of common-law marriages.

4. Same-Sex Marriage: Family law has evolved to recognize and protect the rights of same-sex couples, granting them the same legal rights and benefits as heterosexual couples in marriage or legal

partnerships.

5. Rights and Obligations of Spouses: Family law delineates the rights and obligations of spouses within a marriage or legal partnership. These may include financial support, property division, inheritance rights, decision-making authority, and legal recognition of parental rights and responsibilities.

6. Marriage Dissolution: Family law provides legal procedures for the dissolution of marriages or legal partnerships through divorce, annulment, or legal separation. It addresses the equitable division of marital property and assets and the allocation of parental rights and responsibilities.

7. Prenuptial and Postnuptial Agreements: Family law allows couples to enter into prenuptial or postnuptial agreements to address property and financial matters in the event of divorce or separation. These agreements can provide clarity and protection for both spouses.

8. Marital Rights and Protections: Family law offers various legal protections to married couples, such as spousal privilege, which allows spouses to refuse to testify against each other in certain legal proceedings.

9. Recognition of Marriage across Jurisdictions: Family law deals with the recognition of marriages and legal partnerships performed in different jurisdictions, ensuring consistent legal rights and obligations regardless of where the union took place.

Overall, marriage and legal partnerships play a critical role in family law, as they form the foundation of family relationships and determine the legal status and protections afforded to individuals within these unions. The legal framework surrounding marriage and partnerships continues to evolve to address the diverse needs and rights of individuals in modern society.

Legal requirements for marriage

The legal requirements for marriage can vary depending on the country, state, or jurisdiction in which the marriage takes place. However, some common legal requirements for marriage include:

1. Age of Consent: Both parties must be of the legal age of consent to marry without parental or guardian consent. The age of consent varies between countries and states but is typically 18 years or older.

2. Capacity to Consent: Both parties must have the mental capacity to understand the nature and consequences of marriage. This means they should be able to make informed decisions about getting married and should not be under the influence of drugs or alcohol.

3. No Existing Marriage: Both parties must be unmarried at the time of marriage. Bigamy, or being married to more than one person at the same time, is illegal in most jurisdictions.

4. Consensual Agreement: Both parties must willingly and voluntarily agree to marry each other without any force, coercion, or fraud.

5. Official Ceremony: In most places, a marriage must be performed in a formal ceremony, which may be conducted by a religious leader, civil officiant, or government official.

6. Marriage License: Before the marriage, couples usually need to obtain a marriage license from the appropriate government authority. This license is a legal document

that authorizes the marriage to take place and typically has an expiration date.

7. Witness(es): Some jurisdictions require one or more witnesses to be present during the marriage ceremony to attest to the legality of the marriage.
8. Officiant's Registration: The person officiating the marriage, whether a religious leader or civil officiant, must be registered and authorized to conduct marriages.
9. Legal Documentation: After the marriage ceremony, the officiant is responsible for completing and filing the necessary legal paperwork to register the marriage with the appropriate government authority.

It is essential for couples to familiarize themselves with the specific legal requirements for marriage in their location to ensure a valid and legally recognized union. Additionally, some jurisdictions may have specific rules for international or same-sex marriages, so couples should consult local authorities or legal professionals for guidance if needed.

Rights and responsibilities of spouses

In family law, the rights and responsibilities of spouses refer to the legal obligations and entitlements that each partner in a marriage or civil partnership has towards each other. These rights and responsibilities may vary depending on the jurisdiction and the specific laws governing marriage in that region. However, some common rights and responsibilities of spouses include:

1. Mutual Support and Care: Spouses have a duty to provide emotional and financial support to each other. This includes caring for each other's well-being and contributing to the household's financial stability.
2. Property Rights: In many jurisdictions, spouses have rights to each other's property acquired during the marriage. This may include the right to jointly own property or receive a share of the other spouse's property in case of divorce or death.
3. Inheritance Rights: Spouses often have automatic inheritance rights to each other's estate in the event of one spouse's death, even if there is no will.
4. Right to Live Together: Spouses have the right to live together as a married couple, and usually, neither spouse can force the other to leave the marital home without a court order.
5. Decision-Making: Spouses may have the right to make decisions on each other's behalf in certain situations, such as in medical emergencies or financial matters.
6. Parental Rights and Responsibilities: If the couple has children, both spouses typically have equal rights

and responsibilities regarding the care, custody, and support of their children.

7. Fidelity and Loyalty: Spouses have the expectation of fidelity and loyalty to each other during the marriage.
8. Privacy and Confidentiality: Spouses generally have the right to privacy and confidentiality in their marital communications and interactions.
9. Legal Obligations: Spouses may have legal obligations to each other, such as paying spousal support (alimony) in case of divorce or providing financial assistance to each other.

It is important to note that family law varies widely across different jurisdictions, and the rights and responsibilities of spouses can be influenced by cultural, religious, and social norms. Additionally, some legal rights and responsibilities may be modified or waived through prenuptial or postnuptial agreements. Therefore, it is essential for couples to understand the specific laws and regulations applicable to their marriage and seek legal advice if needed.

Marital agreements and prenuptial agreements

Marital agreements, also known as prenuptial agreements or prenups, are legal contracts entered into by a couple before they get married or enter into a civil partnership. These agreements outline the financial and property rights of each spouse and address how assets and liabilities will be divided in the event of divorce, separation, or the death of one spouse. Marital agreements are an essential aspect of family law, providing couples with a means to protect their individual assets and define their financial expectations during the marriage.

Key aspects of marital agreements include:

1. Financial Disclosure: Both parties must fully disclose their financial assets, debts, and income before creating the agreement. This transparency ensures that each spouse is aware of the other's financial situation.
2. Division of Property: Marital agreements can specify how marital property (acquired during the marriage) and separate property (owned before the marriage) will be divided in the event of divorce or separation.
3. Alimony and Spousal Support: The agreement may address the issue of spousal support or alimony, specifying whether it will be paid and under what conditions.
4. Debts and Liabilities: Marital agreements can determine how joint debts and liabilities will be

handled during the marriage and after a divorce.

5. Inheritance: The agreement may address how inheritance and estate rights will be treated in case of death.
6. Children and Custody: While custody arrangements and child support are generally determined separately from prenuptial agreements, they can include provisions regarding financial support for children.
7. Fairness and Validity: For a prenuptial agreement to be enforceable, it must be fair and meet legal requirements in the jurisdiction where the couple resides. Both parties should have sufficient time to review the agreement and seek legal counsel if needed.

It's essential to understand that prenuptial agreements are not about planning for divorce, but rather about clarifying financial expectations and protecting assets in case of unforeseen circumstances. When drafted with transparency and fairness, prenups can provide peace of mind for both spouses and create a solid foundation for their future together.

However, it is crucial to consult with legal professionals experienced in family law when creating a marital agreement. This ensures that the agreement meets legal requirements and adequately protects the rights and interests of both parties involved.

Recognition of common-law partnerships

Recognition of common-law partnerships refers to the legal acknowledgment of a relationship between two individuals who have lived together for a significant period, typically without being formally married. Common-law partnerships, also known as de facto relationships or cohabitation relationships, vary in their legal recognition and rights depending on the jurisdiction.

In many countries, common-law partnerships are recognized for certain legal purposes, such as:

1. Property Rights: Some jurisdictions provide property rights and entitlements to partners in a common-law relationship, similar to those enjoyed by married couples.
2. Inheritance: In the event of one partner's death, some jurisdictions may grant the surviving partner certain inheritance rights or entitlements to the deceased partner's estate.
3. Medical Decisions: Common-law partners may be given the legal authority to make medical decisions on behalf of their partner, similar to a spouse.
4. Family Benefits: Some government programs, such as social security, health insurance, or parental leave, may extend benefits to partners in common-law relationships.
5. Child Custody and Support: In cases of separation, common-law partners may have rights and responsibilities concerning child custody and support, similar to married couples.

However, the recognition and rights of common-law partnerships vary significantly from one country or state to another. Some jurisdictions offer full legal recognition with almost equal rights to married couples, while others may grant limited rights or no legal recognition at all.

To ensure the rights and entitlements of common-law partners are protected, it is essential for couples to understand the laws in their specific jurisdiction. In some cases, couples may choose to enter into cohabitation agreements or similar legal contracts to clarify their rights and responsibilities during the relationship and in the event of separation.

It is always advisable for individuals in common-law partnerships to seek legal advice from a family lawyer familiar with the laws in their area to understand their legal rights and to address any specific concerns or needs they may have.

Divorce and Dissolution of Marriage

Divorce and dissolution of marriage refer to the legal processes by which a marriage is legally terminated, and the marital relationship is formally ended. These processes allow spouses to legally separate, and they may include resolving various issues such as property division, child custody, child support, and alimony (spousal support). Divorce and dissolution laws can vary significantly from one jurisdiction to another, but some common elements exist in most cases:

1. Petition for Divorce: The process typically begins when one spouse files a petition for divorce or dissolution with the court. This document formally requests the termination of the marriage and outlines the issues to be addressed during the proceedings.

2. Legal Grounds for Divorce: In some jurisdictions, specific legal grounds are required to grant a divorce, such as adultery, cruelty, abandonment, or irreconcilable differences. In other jurisdictions, no-fault divorce allows a marriage to be dissolved without requiring the parties to prove fault.

3. Division of Marital Property: During divorce proceedings, the court will determine how marital property and assets are to be divided between the spouses. Marital property generally includes assets acquired during the marriage, and each jurisdiction may have its own rules for division.

4. Child Custody and Support: If the divorcing couple has children, decisions regarding child custody and visitation arrangements will be made. Child support

may also be established to ensure the financial needs of the children are met.

5. Spousal Support (Alimony): Depending on the jurisdiction and the circumstances of the divorce, one spouse may be ordered to pay alimony (spousal support) to the other for financial support.

6. Settlement or Trial: In some cases, divorcing couples may be able to reach a settlement agreement through negotiation or mediation, resolving all issues related to the divorce. If the parties cannot agree, a trial may be necessary to have the court make decisions on contested matters.

7. Final Decree of Divorce: Once all issues are resolved, the court will issue a final decree of divorce or dissolution, officially ending the marriage.

Divorce and dissolution can be emotionally challenging and legally complex processes. Seeking legal representation from a qualified family lawyer is essential to protect one's rights and interests during the proceedings. Additionally, alternative dispute resolution methods, such as mediation or collaborative divorce, may be options to consider for a more amicable resolution.

Grounds for divorce

Grounds for divorce refer to the legal reasons or justifications recognized by a jurisdiction that allow a married couple to seek a divorce or dissolution of marriage. Different countries and states have their own laws governing divorce, and the grounds for divorce can vary significantly depending on the legal system. Generally, there are two main categories of grounds for divorce:

1. Fault-Based Grounds: In jurisdictions with fault-based divorce laws, one spouse must prove that the other spouse has committed a specific wrongdoing or marital misconduct to obtain a divorce. Common fault-based grounds for divorce may include:

   a. Adultery: One spouse engaging in a sexual relationship outside the marriage. b. Cruelty: Physical or emotional abuse inflicted by one spouse on the other. c. Desertion or Abandonment: One spouse leaving the marital home and refusing to return. d. Substance Abuse: Substance addiction or abuse that significantly impacts the marriage. e. Imprisonment: One spouse being sentenced to a lengthy prison term. f. Mental Incapacity: A spouse being declared legally incompetent or mentally ill.

2. No-Fault Grounds: In jurisdictions with no-fault divorce laws, a couple can seek a divorce without proving any specific wrongdoing by either party. Instead, they can simply state that the marriage has irretrievably broken down, or there are irreconcilable differences. No-fault divorce laws aim to make the divorce process less adversarial and allow couples to end their marriage without blaming one another.

Many jurisdictions have transitioned from fault-based to no-fault divorce laws, and some may offer both options. The availability of fault-based grounds for divorce may vary based on cultural and religious factors. Additionally, in some places, couples may be required to be legally separated for a specific period before filing for a no-fault divorce.

It's important to consult local laws and regulations to understand the specific grounds for divorce in a particular jurisdiction, as they can vary significantly. Moreover, the legal procedures and requirements for divorce, including property division, child custody, and support, may also differ based on the grounds chosen for divorce. Seeking legal advice from a qualified family lawyer is crucial when navigating the divorce process.

Legal processes for divorce and annulment

The legal processes for divorce and annulment are distinct and have different outcomes in family law. Both processes involve the termination of a marriage, but they are based on different grounds and have varying effects on the legal status of the marriage.

1. Divorce:

- Divorce is the legal process by which a married couple ends their marriage, and it is usually based on the irretrievable breakdown of the relationship or irreconcilable differences between the spouses.
- The process of obtaining a divorce varies by jurisdiction, but it typically involves filing a petition for divorce with the appropriate court and serving the divorce papers on the other spouse.
- During the divorce proceedings, various issues such as property division, alimony or spousal support, child custody, and child support are addressed and resolved.
- Once the court grants the divorce, the marriage is legally dissolved, and both parties are free to remarry if they choose to do so.

2. Annulment:

- Annulment is a legal procedure that declares a marriage null and void, as if it never existed. Unlike divorce, which ends a valid marriage, an annulment establishes that the marriage was never legally valid or legally binding from the beginning.

- Annulment is granted based on specific grounds recognized by the jurisdiction. Common grounds for annulment include bigamy (one spouse was already married to another person at the time of the marriage), fraud or misrepresentation (one spouse deceived the other into marriage), lack of consent (one or both parties did not give informed consent to the marriage), or inability to consummate the marriage.
- The process of obtaining an annulment varies by jurisdiction and may involve filing a petition with the court and providing evidence to support the grounds for annulment.
- If the court grants the annulment, the marriage is declared null and void, and it is legally as if the marriage never occurred. This means that parties involved in an annulled marriage are not considered legally married and do not have the legal rights and responsibilities that come with marriage.

It's essential to understand the specific laws and requirements related to divorce and annulment in the relevant jurisdiction, as they can vary significantly. Additionally, seeking legal counsel from a family lawyer is highly recommended to navigate the legal processes and protect one's rights and interests during divorce or annulment proceedings.

Division of assets and property

In family law, the division of assets and property is a crucial aspect of divorce or dissolution of marriage. When a marriage ends, the couple must decide how to fairly divide their marital property, assets, and debts. This process is known as "property division" or "equitable distribution," depending on the jurisdiction.

Here are some key points related to the division of assets and property:

1. Marital vs. Separate Property:
    - Marital property refers to assets and debts acquired during the marriage by either spouse. This can include real estate, bank accounts, vehicles, investments, and other possessions obtained during the marriage.
    - Separate property includes assets that were owned by one spouse before the marriage, gifts or inheritances received by one spouse during the marriage, or any property acquired after the couple's separation.
2. Equitable Distribution:
    - In many jurisdictions, including several U.S. states, the principle of equitable distribution is followed. This means that the court will divide the marital property in a manner it deems fair and equitable, but not necessarily equal.
    - The court considers various factors when determining how to distribute the assets,

including the length of the marriage, each spouse's financial contributions, the value of individual assets, and the needs of each party post-divorce.

3. Community Property:

- In some jurisdictions, such as certain U.S. states and countries, community property laws apply. Under community property principles, all assets and debts acquired during the marriage are considered equally owned by both spouses, and they are divided equally between them during divorce.

4. Property Settlement Agreement:

- Couples have the option to negotiate and agree on the division of assets and debts outside of court through a property settlement agreement. This agreement outlines how the couple intends to divide their property, and it requires court approval.
- A property settlement agreement provides more control to the parties involved, as they can customize the division of assets based on their unique circumstances.

5. Valuation of Assets:

- The value of assets can play a significant role in property division. It is essential to obtain accurate and up-to-date valuations of all assets, including real estate, businesses, and investments.

6. Debts:

- In addition to dividing assets, debts acquired during the marriage are also typically divided between the spouses. This includes mortgages, credit card debt, and other loans.

7. Legal Assistance:

- Given the complexity of property division,

seeking legal counsel from a family lawyer is highly recommended. An experienced attorney can guide individuals through the process, protect their rights, and help them reach a fair settlement.

It's important to remember that property division can be emotionally challenging, but approaching it with a focus on fairness and open communication can lead to a smoother process. Ultimately, the goal is to reach a resolution that allows both parties to move forward with their lives after the dissolution of the marriage.

Spousal support and alimony

Spousal support, commonly known as alimony, is a legal arrangement in family law where one spouse provides financial support to the other spouse after a divorce or legal separation. The purpose of spousal support is to help the lower-earning or non-earning spouse maintain a reasonable standard of living and economic stability post-divorce.

Here are some key points related to spousal support and alimony:

1. Determining Eligibility:
   - The eligibility for spousal support varies based on jurisdiction and the specific circumstances of the case. In general, the spouse seeking support must demonstrate a need for financial assistance, and the other spouse must have the ability to provide support.
2. Factors Considered:
   - Courts consider various factors when determining the amount and duration of spousal support. These may include the length of the marriage, each spouse's financial resources and needs, the standard of living during the marriage, the recipient spouse's ability to become financially self-sufficient, and any contributions made by the recipient spouse to the other spouse's education or career.
3. Types of Spousal Support:

- Different jurisdictions may recognize various types of spousal support arrangements. Temporary support is often granted during the divorce proceedings to maintain financial stability until a final settlement is reached. Permanent or long-term support may be awarded in cases where one spouse is unable to become financially independent due to age, health, or other factors.

4. Duration of Support:
   - The duration of spousal support can vary widely, depending on the circumstances. It can be temporary, lasting only for a specific period, or it may continue indefinitely until certain conditions are met, such as the remarriage of the recipient spouse.

5. Modification and Termination:
   - Spousal support orders can be modified or terminated under certain conditions. If there are substantial changes in either spouse's financial situation or if the recipient spouse becomes financially self-sufficient, the court may adjust or terminate the support order.

6. Tax Implications:
   - The tax treatment of spousal support varies depending on the jurisdiction. In some places, spousal support payments are tax-deductible for the paying spouse and taxable income for the recipient spouse, while in other locations, they are treated differently for tax purposes.

7. Legal Assistance:
   - Given the complexity of spousal support matters, it is advisable for both spouses to seek legal counsel from a family lawyer. An attorney can provide guidance, negotiate on behalf of their client, and ensure that their

rights and interests are protected during the spousal support determination process.

Spousal support is a crucial aspect of divorce proceedings, as it can significantly impact the financial well-being of both parties involved. The aim of the court is to ensure a fair and equitable arrangement that helps the recipient spouse transition to a financially independent life while taking into account the financial capacity of the paying spouse.

Child Custody and Support

Child custody and child support are vital aspects of family law that focus on the well-being and care of children when parents separate or divorce. These legal arrangements ensure that the children's best interests are prioritized and that they continue to receive financial support and emotional care from both parents.

Here are the key points related to child custody and support:

1. Child Custody:
    - Child custody refers to the legal right and responsibility of a parent to make decisions about their child's upbringing, including education, healthcare, and religious practices.
    - There are two main types of child custody: physical custody and legal custody. Physical custody determines where the child will live, while legal custody grants the right to make decisions regarding the child's life.
    - Custody arrangements can be joint, where both parents share decision-making responsibilities, or sole, where one parent has primary custody, and the other parent may have visitation rights.
2. Child Support:
    - Child support is financial assistance provided by one parent to the other for the care and maintenance of their child.
    - The amount of child support is typically determined based on factors such as each parent's income, the number of children, the

custody arrangement, and the child's needs.

- Child support is intended to cover the child's basic necessities, including food, clothing, shelter, education, and healthcare.

3. Custody Agreements and Parenting Plans:
- When parents decide to separate or divorce, they may work together to create a custody agreement or parenting plan that outlines the custody arrangement and visitation schedule.
- Custody agreements should be in the best interests of the child, providing stability and continuity in their daily lives.

4. Child Custody Disputes:
- In some cases, parents may not agree on child custody arrangements, leading to custody disputes. In such situations, the court will step in to determine the custody arrangement based on the child's best interests.
- The court may consider various factors, such as each parent's ability to provide a safe and stable environment, the child's relationship with each parent, and the child's preferences (depending on their age and maturity).

5. Enforcement and Modification:
- Child custody and support orders are legally binding, and failure to comply with them may result in legal consequences.
- In certain situations, such as significant changes in circumstances or the child's needs, custody and support orders may be modified.

6. Parental Rights and Responsibilities:
- Regardless of the custody arrangement, both parents continue to have parental rights and responsibilities toward their child. It is essential for parents to maintain a positive

and supportive relationship with their child even if they do not have physical custody.

Child custody and support are emotionally charged topics, and decisions made during this process can have a long-lasting impact on children and parents alike. It is essential for parents to approach these matters with sensitivity, cooperation, and the child's best interests at heart. Seeking legal counsel from a family lawyer can provide valuable guidance and ensure that the rights of both parents and the well-being of the child are protected throughout the process.

Types of child custody arrangements

In family law, child custody arrangements refer to the legal and physical custody of a child after the parents separate or divorce. There are several types of child custody arrangements, and the specific arrangement chosen will depend on the parents' and the court's consideration of the child's best interests. Here are the most common types of child custody arrangements:

1. Joint Physical Custody:
   - In joint physical custody, the child spends significant time living with both parents. The child may alternate living with each parent on a regular schedule, such as weekly or bi-weekly.
   - This arrangement aims to provide the child with frequent and continuing contact with both parents, allowing them to maintain strong relationships with each.

2. Sole Physical Custody:
   - In sole physical custody, the child primarily lives with one parent, and the other parent is granted visitation rights or parenting time.
   - The custodial parent is responsible for the child's day-to-day care, and the non-custodial parent typically has scheduled visitation.

3. Joint Legal Custody:
   - Joint legal custody refers to both parents sharing decision-making authority for major life decisions concerning the child, such as education, healthcare, and religious

upbringing.

- Even if the child primarily lives with one parent, both parents have equal input in making important decisions affecting the child's life.

4. Sole Legal Custody:

- In sole legal custody, one parent has the exclusive right to make major decisions regarding the child's upbringing.
- The parent with sole legal custody is solely responsible for making decisions related to the child's education, healthcare, religion, and other important matters.

5. Bird's Nest Custody:

- In this less common arrangement, the child remains in the family home, and the parents take turns living there and caring for the child on a rotating basis.
- The parents have separate living arrangements when they are not caring for the child.

6. Split Custody:

- Split custody is a less common arrangement where two or more children from the same family are split between the parents, with each parent having primary physical custody of one or more of the children.
- This arrangement is not as common and is typically only considered if it is in the best interests of the children involved.

It's important to note that child custody arrangements can be customized based on the unique circumstances of each family. The primary goal of the court in determining custody is to ensure the child's best interests are met, taking into account factors such as the child's age, emotional and physical needs, the parents' ability to provide a stable environment, the child's relationship with each parent, and any special considerations specific to the child's situation. In some cases, parents may agree on a custody arrangement through mediation or negotiations outside of court, while in other cases, a court may make the decision if the parents cannot agree.

Determining the best interests of the child

Determining the best interests of the child is a fundamental principle in family law when making decisions about child custody and visitation arrangements. The best interests standard is used by courts to ensure that the well-being and welfare of the child are prioritized above all else when making these important decisions. It involves considering various factors that can influence the child's physical, emotional, and psychological health and development.

The specific factors considered may vary depending on the jurisdiction and the unique circumstances of each case, but some common factors include:

1. Child's Age and Developmental Needs: The age and developmental stage of the child are essential factors. Younger children may require more frequent and consistent contact with each parent, while older children may have preferences and opinions that should be considered.

2. Emotional and Physical Health: The mental and physical well-being of the child is crucial. Courts will assess the child's overall health and whether any particular custody arrangement would meet their medical and emotional needs.

3. Stability and Continuity: Courts often consider which parent can provide a stable and consistent environment for the child. Disruptions to the child's routine and frequent changes in living arrangements may not be in the child's best interests.

4. Relationship with Parents and Others: The quality

of the child's relationship with each parent is vital. Courts will consider the level of involvement and bonding with both parents and the child's extended family, as well as any potential caregivers.

5. History of Parental Involvement: The court may review each parent's history of involvement in the child's life, including their roles in caregiving, education, and extracurricular activities.

6. Parental Ability and Willingness: The court will assess each parent's ability and willingness to meet the child's needs, provide a safe and nurturing environment, and facilitate a positive relationship with the other parent.

7. Sibling and Family Relationships: If there are siblings involved, the court may consider the importance of maintaining sibling relationships and ensuring the child's best interests are met in the context of the entire family.

8. Safety and Protection: The child's safety is paramount. Courts will consider any history of abuse or neglect and take steps to protect the child from harmful situations.

9. Parental Cooperation: The willingness of each parent to cooperate and communicate effectively in co-parenting is an essential factor in determining the child's best interests.

It's important to note that the best interests of the child can be a complex and subjective determination. Judges, mediators, and other professionals involved in custody cases carefully assess all relevant factors to make informed decisions that prioritize the child's well-being. In some cases, the court may appoint a guardian ad litem or custody evaluator to provide additional insights into the child's best interests.

Ultimately, the goal of determining the child's best interests is to ensure that the child's physical, emotional, and psychological needs are met and that they can maintain healthy relationships with both parents whenever possible.

Child support guidelines and calculations

Child support guidelines and calculations vary by jurisdiction, but they generally aim to ensure that the financial needs of the child are met by both parents in proportion to their respective incomes. The guidelines consider factors such as the parents' incomes, the number of children, and the parenting arrangement (custodial or non-custodial).

Here's a general overview of how child support calculations are typically done:

1. Income Determination: Both parents' incomes are assessed, which may include wages, salaries, bonuses, commissions, and other sources of income.
2. Deductions: Certain deductions, such as taxes, mandatory retirement contributions, and union dues, may be taken from the parents' gross income to arrive at their net income.
3. Basic Child Support Obligation: The court or relevant agency refers to a child support table or guideline that outlines the basic support obligation based on the parents' combined income and the number of children they have.
4. Proportional Share: Each parent's proportionate share of the total child support obligation is determined based on their individual income contribution to the combined income.
5. Additional Expenses: In addition to the basic support obligation, certain additional expenses may be considered, such as child care costs, health insurance premiums, and extraordinary medical expenses.

6. Parenting Time Adjustment: In some cases, the amount of child support may be adjusted based on the parenting time each parent has with the child. If one parent has more parenting time than the other, their child support obligation may be reduced.

7. Deviation Factors: In certain situations, the court may deviate from the standard child support guidelines if there are special circumstances, such as the child's extraordinary medical needs or the financial resources of the parents.

Once these calculations are made, the court will typically issue an order outlining the amount of child support that the non-custodial parent (the parent with whom the child does not primarily reside) must pay to the custodial parent (the parent with whom the child primarily resides).

It's essential to remember that child support is intended to benefit the child and ensure that they have access to the financial resources necessary for their well-being. The guidelines and calculations are meant to provide a fair and reasonable amount based on the parents' incomes and the needs of the child. However, circumstances can change over time, and child support orders can be modified if there are significant changes in the parents' financial situations or the child's needs.

Child custody modifications and enforcement

Child custody modifications and enforcement are essential aspects of family law that come into play when there are changes in circumstances or when one parent fails to comply with the custody order. Here's an overview of these concepts:

1. Child Custody Modifications:
    - Changes in Circumstances: Child custody orders are generally based on the best interests of the child at the time of the original order. However, circumstances can change over time, such as a parent's relocation, a change in work schedule, or a significant change in the child's needs or preferences.
    - Petition for Modification: If a parent seeks to modify the existing custody arrangement, they can file a petition with the family court. They must demonstrate a substantial change in circumstances that justifies modifying the existing custody order.
2. Mediation and Negotiation:
    - Before resorting to court, parents may attempt mediation or negotiation to reach an agreement on custody modifications. Mediation involves a neutral third party helping the parents work through the issues, while negotiation involves direct communication between the parents with or without legal representation.

3. Court Proceedings:
   - If parents cannot agree on custody modifications, they may need to go through court proceedings. The court will consider the child's best interests when making a decision, taking into account factors such as the child's age, preferences, relationships with each parent, and the ability of each parent to meet the child's needs.
4. Custody Enforcement:
   - Non-Compliance: If a parent fails to adhere to the custody order, the other parent can seek enforcement through the family court. Non-compliance may involve denial of visitation rights or refusal to return the child after visitation.
   - Legal Remedies: The court has various remedies to enforce the custody order, such as fines, make-up visitation time, modification of the existing order, and, in severe cases, contempt of court.
5. Mediation for Enforcement:
   - Sometimes, mediation can also be used to address custody enforcement issues. A mediator can assist the parents in finding practical solutions to ensure compliance with the custody order.

It's essential to work with experienced family law professionals, such as attorneys and mediators, to navigate custody modifications and enforcement effectively. Open communication and a focus on the child's best interests can help parents resolve disputes and maintain a healthy co-parenting relationship even in challenging situations.

Adoption and Surrogacy

Adoption and surrogacy are important aspects of family law that involve creating or expanding a family through legal means. Here's an overview of adoption and surrogacy:

1. Adoption:

   - Types of Adoption: Adoption can occur through various methods, including domestic adoption (within the country) and international adoption (from another country). It can also be open, semi-open, or closed, depending on the level of contact between birth parents, adoptive parents, and the child.
   - Legal Process: The adoption process involves a series of legal steps, including home studies, background checks, parental rights termination (in some cases), and finalization in court. The court's final order legally establishes the adoptive parents as the child's legal parents.
   - Adoption Agencies: Many adoptions are facilitated through licensed adoption agencies that work with both birth parents and adoptive parents to match them based on compatibility and preferences.

2. Surrogacy:

   - Types of Surrogacy: Surrogacy can be traditional (using the surrogate's own egg) or gestational (using a donor egg or the intended mother's egg). Gestational surrogacy is more common and does not involve a genetic connection between the surrogate and the child.

- Legal Process: Surrogacy involves complex legal agreements between the intended parents and the surrogate, specifying the rights and responsibilities of each party. The legal process varies depending on the jurisdiction, as some countries or states have specific regulations or restrictions regarding surrogacy.

- Medical and Emotional Support: Throughout the surrogacy journey, intended parents and surrogates receive medical and emotional support to ensure the well-being of both parties and the baby.

3. Legal Protections:

- In both adoption and surrogacy, legal protections are in place to safeguard the rights of all involved parties. These protections ensure that the child's best interests are prioritized, and the rights and responsibilities of the parents and the child are legally recognized.

4. Emotional Considerations:

- Adoption and surrogacy are profound emotional journeys for all parties involved. Birth parents, adoptive parents, surrogates, and the child may experience a range of emotions throughout the process. Emotional support and counseling are often available to help individuals navigate these emotions.

5. LGBTQ+ Families:

- Adoption and surrogacy have been significant pathways for LGBTQ+ families to build their families. Legal advancements in many jurisdictions have recognized the rights of same-sex couples and LGBTQ+ individuals to adopt and pursue surrogacy.

Adoption and surrogacy are beautiful ways to form families and bring joy to individuals and couples seeking to become parents. While the legal processes can be complex, the end result is the creation of loving families and the nurturing of new lives. It's important to work with experienced professionals, such as adoption agencies and surrogacy agencies, as well as family law attorneys, to ensure a smooth and legally sound process.

Legal requirements and procedures for adoption

The legal requirements and procedures for adoption vary depending on the country or state in which the adoption takes place. However, some common steps and requirements in the adoption process include:

1. Research and Orientation: Prospective adoptive parents typically begin the process by researching adoption options and attending orientation sessions or informational meetings provided by adoption agencies or adoption organizations.

2. Home Study: A home study is a crucial part of the adoption process. It involves a thorough assessment of the prospective adoptive parents' home, background checks, interviews, and evaluations to ensure their suitability to adopt a child.

3. Adoption Application: After completing the home study, prospective adoptive parents submit an adoption application to the adoption agency or relevant authorities. This application includes personal information, references, and other required documents.

4. Matching and Placement: Once approved, prospective adoptive parents may go through a matching process where they are matched with a child whose needs and characteristics align with their family's profile. After the match, the child is placed in the adoptive home.

5. Post-Placement Visits: After the child is placed with

the adoptive family, post-placement visits may be conducted to assess the child's adjustment and well-being.

6. Termination of Parental Rights: In cases of domestic adoption, the parental rights of the child's birth parents must be terminated legally before the adoption can be finalized.

7. Consent and Relinquishment: Birth parents may provide consent or relinquishment of their parental rights voluntarily or as mandated by the court.

8. Finalization: After a specified waiting period, and if the adoption process meets all legal requirements, a court hearing is held to finalize the adoption. The court then issues an adoption decree or order, officially establishing the adoptive parents as the child's legal parents.

9. Adoption Certificate: Following the finalization, an adoption certificate or decree is issued as legal proof of the adoption.

It's essential to work with a licensed adoption agency or adoption attorney to ensure compliance with all legal requirements and navigate the adoption process smoothly. International adoptions may involve additional legal considerations, including immigration and international adoption laws. As adoption laws can be complex, it's crucial to seek legal advice and assistance from professionals experienced in adoption matters.

Open adoption and closed adoption

Open adoption and closed adoption are two different types of adoption arrangements that involve varying degrees of communication and contact between birth parents, adoptive parents, and the adopted child. Here's a brief overview of each:

1. Open Adoption: In an open adoption, there is an ongoing exchange of identifying information and direct communication between the birth parents, adoptive parents, and the adopted child. The level of openness can vary widely based on the preferences of all parties involved and may include regular visits, phone calls, emails, or letters. Open adoption allows for greater transparency and often fosters a positive relationship between birth parents and adoptive parents, providing the child with an understanding of their adoption story and the opportunity to maintain connections with their birth family.

2. Closed Adoption: In a closed adoption, there is no contact or exchange of identifying information between the birth parents and the adoptive parents. The identities of both parties may remain confidential, and the child is typically unaware of their birth parents' identities. In a closed adoption, the adoption agency or court acts as an intermediary, and all communication is kept confidential. Closed adoptions were more common in the past, but their prevalence has decreased as open adoption has become more widely accepted.

It's important to note that there is also a middle ground known as semi-open adoption or mediated adoption, which combines elements of both open and closed adoption. In a semi-open adoption, communication and contact are facilitated through an intermediary (such as an adoption agency), allowing for the exchange of non-identifying information and sometimes mediated visits.

The choice between open and closed adoption is deeply personal and depends on the preferences and comfort levels of the birth parents, adoptive parents, and the child involved. Some people may prefer the increased communication and transparency of open adoption, while others may feel more comfortable with a closed or semi-open arrangement. Adoption agencies and adoption professionals can help prospective birth parents and adoptive parents explore their options and make informed decisions that align with their individual needs and desires.

Surrogacy agreements and legal parentage

Surrogacy agreements involve a legal arrangement between intended parents (individuals or couples) and a surrogate mother to carry and give birth to a child on their behalf. In surrogacy, there are two main types: traditional surrogacy and gestational surrogacy.

1. Traditional Surrogacy: In traditional surrogacy, the surrogate mother is genetically related to the child because her own eggs are used in the conception process. In this arrangement, the surrogate is both the biological mother and the gestational carrier. Traditional surrogacy is less common and can raise complex legal and emotional issues.
2. Gestational Surrogacy: In gestational surrogacy, the surrogate mother is not genetically related to the child. Instead, an embryo created through in vitro fertilization (IVF) using the intended mother's eggs and the intended father's sperm (or donor gametes) is implanted into the surrogate's uterus. In this case, the surrogate is only the gestational carrier, and the intended parents are the genetic parents of the child.

Legal parentage in surrogacy agreements varies by jurisdiction, and laws may differ significantly from one place to another. Some countries and states have specific laws regulating surrogacy, while others may have no legal framework or ambiguous laws on the matter.

Legal parentage is typically established through a court process that may involve a pre-birth order or a post-birth legal proceeding. The pre-birth order allows the intended parents' names to be listed on the birth certificate immediately upon the child's birth, while a post-birth legal proceeding may require the intended parents to adopt the child after birth.

It's crucial for all parties involved in a surrogacy agreement to consult with legal professionals specializing in family law and reproductive law to understand the legal implications and protections specific to their jurisdiction. Additionally, surrogacy agreements should be comprehensive and clearly outline the rights and responsibilities of all parties, including financial arrangements, medical decisions, and potential contingencies.

Given the complexity and variation in surrogacy laws, it is essential for intended parents and surrogate mothers to work closely with experienced professionals to ensure a smooth and legally sound surrogacy journey.

International adoption and legal considerations

International adoption involves the process of adopting a child from a foreign country and bringing them to the adoptive parents' home country. While international adoption can be a beautiful way to build a family and provide a loving home to a child in need, it comes with its own set of legal considerations and challenges. Here are some key legal aspects to consider in international adoption:

1. Adoption Laws and Regulations: Each country has its own set of adoption laws and regulations, and they can vary significantly. It is essential to research and understand the adoption requirements of both the adoptive parents' home country and the country from which they plan to adopt. International adoption agencies and legal professionals with expertise in international adoption can provide guidance through this process.

2. Eligibility and Requirements: Adoptive parents must meet specific eligibility criteria set by the adoptive country. Requirements may include age, marital status, financial stability, medical conditions, and more. Some countries also have specific requirements related to the age and number of children in the prospective adoptive parents' home.

3. Home Study: In most international adoptions, the adoptive parents are required to undergo a home study, which is an assessment of their suitability as

adoptive parents. The home study typically includes interviews, background checks, and home visits by a social worker or adoption professional.

4. Hague Convention on Protection of Children and Co-operation in Respect of Intercountry Adoption: The Hague Adoption Convention is an international treaty aimed at protecting the rights and welfare of children in international adoption. Some countries are parties to the Convention, while others are not. Adoptions from Hague Convention countries must adhere to specific procedures, including the use of accredited adoption agencies.

5. Immigration and Visa Requirements: Adoptive parents must comply with the immigration and visa requirements of both the adoptive country and the home country to bring the adopted child legally into their home country.

6. Post-Adoption Reporting: Many countries require adoptive parents to submit post-adoption reports at regular intervals to ensure the well-being and adjustment of the adopted child.

7. Dual Citizenship and Legal Recognition: Depending on the countries involved, the adopted child may acquire dual citizenship. It is essential to understand the legal implications of dual citizenship and ensure that the child's adoption is recognized in both countries.

8. Legal Representation: International adoption can be a complex legal process, and adoptive parents should seek legal representation from professionals experienced in international adoption laws and regulations.

International adoption is a rewarding journey, but it requires careful planning, thorough research, and compliance with the legal requirements of both the adoptive country and the country of origin. Prospective adoptive parents should work closely with adoption agencies, legal experts, and immigration authorities to navigate the process smoothly and ethically.

LGBTQ+ Rights and Family Law

LGBTQ+ rights and family law have been significant areas of legal and social development in recent years. As societies evolve and embrace more inclusive perspectives, legal systems around the world have worked to address the unique family dynamics and challenges faced by LGBTQ+ individuals and couples. Here are some key aspects of LGBTQ+ rights and family law:

1. Marriage Equality: One of the most significant milestones in LGBTQ+ rights has been the recognition of same-sex marriage in many countries. Marriage equality allows LGBTQ+ couples to legally marry and enjoy the same rights and benefits as opposite-sex couples, including access to spousal benefits, inheritance rights, and parental rights.

2. Adoption and Parental Rights: LGBTQ+ individuals and couples have fought for and won the right to adopt children in many jurisdictions. Legal recognition of same-sex parents has become more widespread, and LGBTQ+ parents can now secure legal rights and responsibilities for their children through adoption or other legal means.

3. Parentage and Surrogacy: In some jurisdictions, there may be complexities around parentage for LGBTQ + individuals or couples who use surrogacy to have children. It is essential to navigate the legal landscape and ensure that all parental rights are recognized and protected.

4. Fertility and Reproductive Rights: Access to assisted reproductive technologies, such as in vitro

fertilization (IVF) and artificial insemination, has expanded options for LGBTQ+ individuals and couples who wish to become parents biologically.

5. Divorce and Dissolution: Just as LGBTQ+ couples have gained the right to marry, they also have the right to divorce or dissolve their marriages. Legal processes for divorce, property division, and child custody are available to LGBTQ+ couples on an equal basis.

6. Transgender and Non-Binary Rights: Legal recognition of gender identity is another crucial aspect of LGBTQ+ rights. Many countries have developed legal frameworks for individuals to change their gender marker on official documents and access gender-affirming healthcare.

7. Discrimination Protections: Anti-discrimination laws and policies aim to protect LGBTQ+ individuals from discrimination in various areas of life, including employment, housing, and public services.

8. Religious Exemptions: In some jurisdictions, there may be religious exemptions that allow certain institutions or individuals to refuse services to LGBTQ+ individuals or couples based on their religious beliefs. Balancing religious freedom with the protection of LGBTQ+ rights remains a complex and evolving issue.

9. Legal Challenges and Progress: Despite significant progress, challenges persist, and LGBTQ+ rights continue to be a subject of legal and social debates in some parts of the world. Legal battles and advocacy efforts play a crucial role in advancing equality and justice for LGBTQ+ individuals and families.

LGBTQ+ rights and family law continue to evolve as societies strive for greater inclusivity and equality. Legal systems play a critical role in recognizing and protecting the rights of LGBTQ+ individuals and families, ensuring that they have equal access to

family-related rights and benefits.

Same-sex marriage and legal recognition

Same-sex marriage refers to the marriage between two individuals of the same gender or sex. Over the past few decades, the legal recognition of same-sex marriage has been a significant milestone in the global fight for LGBTQ+ rights. Here are some key points about same-sex marriage and its legal recognition:

1. Historical Context: Same-sex relationships have existed throughout history, but legal recognition and acceptance have varied across different cultures and time periods. In recent times, the struggle for same-sex marriage rights gained momentum as LGBTQ+ individuals and advocacy groups sought equality and recognition of their relationships under the law.

2. Marriage Equality Movement: The marriage equality movement, which gained widespread attention in the late 20th and early 21st centuries, sought to secure the legal right for same-sex couples to marry. The movement focused on challenging discriminatory laws and advocating for equal rights and treatment for LGBTQ+ individuals.

3. Legalization Around the World: As of my knowledge cutoff in September 2021, many countries have legalized same-sex marriage, either through legislation or court decisions. Some of the countries that have recognized same-sex marriage include Canada, the United States, the United Kingdom, Germany, Australia, South Africa, and several others.

4. Legal Benefits: Legalizing same-sex marriage provides LGBTQ+ couples with the same legal benefits and

protections as opposite-sex couples. These benefits include inheritance rights, access to health care and insurance, parental rights and responsibilities, tax benefits, and immigration rights, among others.

5. Opposition and Challenges: Despite the progress made in many countries, there are still regions and societies where same-sex marriage faces strong opposition based on religious, cultural, or conservative beliefs. Some countries criminalize same-sex relationships or have laws explicitly prohibiting same-sex marriage.

6. Continuing Advocacy: The fight for same-sex marriage and LGBTQ+ rights continues in many parts of the world. Advocacy groups, activists, and allies work to promote equality, challenge discriminatory laws, and create safe and inclusive spaces for LGBTQ+ individuals and couples.

7. Transnational Recognition: In some cases, same-sex marriages performed in one country may not be recognized in another. This lack of transnational recognition can create legal complexities for LGBTQ+ couples who travel or live in countries where same-sex marriage is not legal or recognized.

8. Ongoing Developments: The legal landscape surrounding same-sex marriage continues to evolve. New countries may legalize same-sex marriage, and existing laws may be amended or challenged through legal processes.

Legal recognition of same-sex marriage represents a significant step toward equality and social acceptance for LGBTQ+ individuals and couples. It reflects a growing understanding of the importance of recognizing and valuing diverse forms of relationships in society. However, the struggle for LGBTQ+ rights extends beyond marriage equality, and efforts to combat discrimination and promote inclusivity continue on various fronts.

LGBTQ+ parenting and adoption rights

LGBTQ+ parenting and adoption rights refer to the legal recognition and protection of same-sex couples and individuals as parents, as well as their right to adopt children. Over the years, there have been significant strides in many countries to acknowledge and uphold the parenting rights of LGBTQ+ individuals and couples. Here are some key points about LGBTQ + parenting and adoption rights:

1. Legal Recognition: LGBTQ+ parents seek the same legal recognition and rights as heterosexual parents. This includes the right to make decisions for their children, access to healthcare and education, and protection under family law.

2. Adoption Rights: Adoption is the legal process by which individuals or couples become the legal parents of a child who is not their biological child. Many countries now allow LGBTQ+ individuals and couples to adopt children, recognizing that sexual orientation or gender identity does not affect one's ability to be a loving and capable parent.

3. Foster Care: LGBTQ+ individuals and couples are increasingly welcomed as foster parents, providing temporary care for children in need until a permanent home can be found. Foster care agencies are moving towards inclusive policies that promote diversity and support LGBTQ+ parents.

4. Second-Parent Adoption: In cases where one partner in a same-sex couple is the biological or legal parent of a child, the other partner may pursue second-

parent adoption to gain legal parental rights. This process ensures both parents have legal rights and responsibilities regarding the child.

5. Surrogacy and Assisted Reproduction: LGBTQ+ individuals and couples may also choose surrogacy or assisted reproduction to have children. This involves using a surrogate mother to carry the pregnancy or using donor sperm or eggs in assisted reproductive procedures.

6. Challenges and Discrimination: Despite progress, LGBTQ+ parents may still face challenges related to discrimination and prejudice. This can manifest in legal obstacles, bias in adoption processes, or societal attitudes that stigmatize non-traditional families.

7. Transnational Adoption: For LGBTQ+ couples considering adoption from other countries, it's essential to understand the laws and cultural attitudes towards LGBTQ+ parenting in both the adopting country and the child's country of origin.

8. Ongoing Advocacy: Advocacy organizations and LGBTQ+ rights activists continue to work towards greater recognition and protection of parenting rights for LGBTQ+ individuals and families. They seek to dismantle discriminatory policies and promote inclusive and supportive family laws.

9. Positive Impact: Research has shown that children raised by LGBTQ+ parents fare as well as children raised by heterosexual parents. Studies indicate that parental sexual orientation or gender identity does not significantly impact a child's well-being, with the key determinant being a supportive and loving family environment.

As society becomes more inclusive and accepting, many countries are recognizing and affirming the parenting rights of LGBTQ+ individuals and couples. These legal advances contribute to greater equality and social acceptance for diverse families and underscore the importance of providing a nurturing and loving environment for all children, regardless of their parents' sexual orientation or gender identity.

Family law challenges and advancements for LGBTQ+ couples

Family law challenges and advancements for LGBTQ+ couples have been significant and varied over the years. While there have been notable advances in many countries, there are still areas of concern and ongoing work to ensure equal rights and protections for LGBTQ+ families. Here are some key challenges and advancements in family law for LGBTQ+ couples:

Challenges:

1. Legal Recognition: One of the primary challenges has been the legal recognition of same-sex relationships and families. Historically, many countries did not recognize same-sex marriages or partnerships, which led to limited legal rights and protections for LGBTQ+ couples and their children.

2. Adoption and Surrogacy: Adoption and surrogacy processes have often presented obstacles for LGBTQ+ couples. Some countries restricted same-sex couples' adoption rights, making it difficult for them to become legal parents. Similarly, surrogacy laws and access to assisted reproductive technologies have been inconsistent and discriminatory in some places.

3. Parental Rights: LGBTQ+ parents have faced challenges regarding legal parental rights, particularly in cases of separation or divorce. Some jurisdictions did not automatically grant legal rights to both parents in same-sex couples, leading to issues related to child

custody and visitation.

4. Healthcare and Parenting: Access to healthcare and parenting rights for LGBTQ+ families has also been a challenge. Some medical institutions may not recognize non-biological parents, making it difficult to make medical decisions for their children.

Advancements:

1. Marriage Equality: One of the most significant advancements has been the recognition of same-sex marriages in many countries. Legalizing same-sex marriage has granted LGBTQ+ couples the same rights and protections as heterosexual couples, including inheritance rights, joint tax filing, and spousal benefits.

2. Adoption Rights: Many countries have made strides in recognizing the right of LGBTQ+ individuals and couples to adopt children. Adoption laws have been updated to be more inclusive, allowing same-sex couples to adopt children and provide loving homes for those in need.

3. Surrogacy and Assisted Reproduction: Advancements in assisted reproductive technologies and surrogacy laws have provided LGBTQ+ couples with more options for starting families and having biological children.

4. Parental Rights: In many jurisdictions, parental rights have been expanded to ensure that both parents in a same-sex couple have equal rights and responsibilities towards their children.

5. Healthcare Equality: Laws and policies have been updated to ensure that LGBTQ+ parents have equal access to healthcare for their children, with legal recognition and decision-making authority.

6. Anti-Discrimination Protections: Some countries have

enacted anti-discrimination laws to protect LGBTQ
+ families from discrimination in various areas,
including housing, education, and public services.
7. International Recognition: There has been increased
international recognition of same-sex marriages and
families, which has facilitated the movement of
LGBTQ+ families across borders with legal protections.
8. Advocacy and Awareness: Ongoing advocacy efforts
by LGBTQ+ rights organizations and activists have
helped raise awareness about the challenges faced by
LGBTQ+ families, leading to policy changes and legal
advancements.

While there have been significant advancements in family law
for LGBTQ+ couples, there is still work to be done to achieve
full equality and recognition in all jurisdictions. Continued
advocacy and legal reforms are essential to ensure that all
families, regardless of sexual orientation or gender identity, are
treated with fairness, respect, and equal protection under the
law.

Family Law and Reproductive Technologies

Family law and reproductive technologies are intricately connected as advancements in assisted reproductive technologies (ART) have raised various legal and ethical questions surrounding parentage, custody, and rights in modern family structures. Here are some key aspects of the intersection between family law and reproductive technologies:

1. Assisted Reproductive Technologies (ART): ART includes various medical procedures that assist individuals and couples in achieving pregnancy, such as in vitro fertilization (IVF), intrauterine insemination (IUI), and egg/sperm donation. These technologies have expanded family-building options but have also posed legal challenges related to parental rights, custody, and financial responsibility.

2. Parental Rights and Legal Parentage: With ART, determining legal parentage can be complex, especially in cases involving third-party donors or surrogacy. Family law must address issues like establishing legal parent-child relationships, parental rights, and responsibilities, and the rights of donors and surrogates.

3. Surrogacy: Surrogacy arrangements involve a woman carrying and giving birth to a child on behalf of another individual or couple. Family law must address the legal recognition of the intended parents, the surrogate's rights and responsibilities, and the

protection of the child's best interests.

4. Donor-Conceived Children: When gamete or embryo donation is used in ART, the legal status of donor-conceived children becomes critical. Family law must address issues of disclosure, the rights of donors and recipients, and the child's access to information about their genetic origins.

5. Same-Sex Parenting: ART has provided same-sex couples with the ability to become parents, leading to legal questions concerning joint parentage, adoption, and the recognition of non-biological parents' rights.

6. Multiple Parenthood: In cases of egg/sperm donation or surrogacy, a child may have multiple legal parents, such as intended parents and donors/surrogates. Family law must address how these complex family structures are legally recognized and protected.

7. Embryo Disposition and Consent: Disputes may arise over the disposition of cryopreserved embryos in cases of divorce or separation. Family law must address consent and decision-making regarding the use, donation, or disposal of frozen embryos.

8. Posthumous Reproduction: Posthumous reproduction involves using gametes from a deceased individual to conceive a child. Family law must address issues like consent, inheritance rights, and the legal status of the child born after the parent's death.

9. International Surrogacy and Cross-Border Issues: ART often involves international surrogacy arrangements, leading to complex legal issues concerning citizenship, travel, and parentage across different jurisdictions.

10. Regulation and Oversight: Family law must navigate the ethical and legal considerations of regulating ART practices, ensuring the protection of all parties involved, including donors, surrogates, intended parents, and the children born through these technologies.

As reproductive technologies continue to advance, family law will need to adapt and evolve to address the legal complexities and protect the rights and interests of all individuals and families involved. Legal frameworks must strike a balance between promoting access to family-building options and ensuring the well-being and protection of the children born through these technologies.

Assisted reproductive technologies (ART)

Assisted Reproductive Technologies (ART) refer to medical procedures or interventions that assist individuals and couples in achieving pregnancy when natural conception is not possible or successful. These technologies have revolutionized the field of reproductive medicine and expanded family-building options for people facing infertility or other reproductive challenges. Some of the most common ART procedures include:

1. In Vitro Fertilization (IVF): IVF is a process where eggs are retrieved from the ovaries and fertilized with sperm in a laboratory dish. The resulting embryos are then transferred to the woman's uterus, increasing the chances of pregnancy.

2. Intrauterine Insemination (IUI): IUI involves placing sperm directly into the woman's uterus to facilitate fertilization. It is commonly used in cases of mild male factor infertility or when the woman has difficulty conceiving.

3. Intracytoplasmic Sperm Injection (ICSI): ICSI is a specialized form of IVF where a single sperm is directly injected into an egg to achieve fertilization. It is commonly used in cases of severe male factor infertility.

4. Egg Donation: Egg donation involves using eggs from a donor to be fertilized with sperm and transferred to the recipient's uterus. This is commonly used when a woman cannot produce viable eggs.

5. Sperm Donation: Sperm donation is the process of using donor sperm to fertilize a woman's egg. It is commonly used when a male partner has fertility issues or when there is no male partner involved.

6. Surrogacy: Surrogacy is an arrangement where a woman (the surrogate) carries and gives birth to a child on behalf of another person or couple (the intended parents). It is commonly used when the intended mother cannot carry a pregnancy or when there are other medical reasons that prevent pregnancy.

7. Embryo Adoption: Embryo adoption involves using donated embryos from couples who have undergone IVF but no longer need the embryos. The embryos are transferred to the recipient's uterus for pregnancy.

8. Cryopreservation (Freezing): ART often involves the cryopreservation of embryos, eggs, or sperm for future use. This allows individuals and couples to preserve their fertility and have the option to use the stored reproductive materials later.

ART has significantly improved the chances of conception and pregnancy for many individuals and couples. However, it also raises various ethical, legal, and social considerations, such as the rights and responsibilities of donors, surrogates, and intended parents, as well as the well-being of children born through these technologies. As a result, regulations and guidelines vary between countries and states to ensure the ethical and safe use of ART while protecting the rights of all parties involved.

Legal implications of surrogacy and egg/sperm donation

Surrogacy and egg/sperm donation can have complex legal implications, as they involve multiple parties and the creation of new legal relationships. The legal considerations can vary depending on the jurisdiction and the specific circumstances of the arrangement. Here are some common legal implications of surrogacy and egg/sperm donation:

1. Parental Rights: In surrogacy arrangements, the legal status of the intended parents and the surrogate mother must be clearly defined. In some jurisdictions, the surrogate mother may have parental rights initially, and a legal process called "parentage order" may be required to transfer parental rights to the intended parents.

2. Consent and Agreements: Comprehensive legal agreements are often drafted to outline the rights and responsibilities of all parties involved, including the intended parents, the surrogate, and the egg/sperm donor. These agreements typically address issues such as parental rights, financial arrangements, confidentiality, and potential risks.

3. Birth Certificates: Depending on the jurisdiction, the birth certificate may list the surrogate mother as the legal mother of the child, even if she has no genetic connection to the child. Parentage orders or adoption proceedings may be necessary to amend the birth certificate and legally recognize the intended parents

as the child's legal parents.

4. Donor Anonymity: Some jurisdictions allow for anonymous egg or sperm donation, while others require the disclosure of donor identity to the child once they reach a certain age. Legal requirements regarding donor anonymity and disclosure vary by region.

5. Inheritance and Estate Planning: Surrogacy and egg/sperm donation may have implications for inheritance and estate planning, as the legal relationship between the child and the intended parents may differ from a biological child.

6. Citizenship and Immigration: In cases where surrogacy or egg/sperm donation involves parties from different countries, there may be implications for citizenship and immigration status for the child and the intended parents.

7. Health and Medical Decisions: Surrogacy agreements often include provisions regarding medical decisions for both the surrogate and the child, especially in the case of unexpected medical issues during the pregnancy or after birth.

8. Health Insurance: Surrogacy and egg/sperm donation arrangements may have implications for health insurance coverage for the surrogate and the child.

Given the complexity of the legal implications, it is essential for all parties involved in surrogacy and egg/sperm donation arrangements to seek legal counsel to ensure that their rights and interests are protected. Additionally, parties should be aware of the laws and regulations specific to their jurisdiction, as they can significantly impact the legal status of the child and the parental rights of the intended parents.

Parental rights and legal parentage in ART cases

Parental rights and legal parentage in Assisted Reproductive Technology (ART) cases can vary depending on the jurisdiction and the specific circumstances of the arrangement. Here are some key aspects of parental rights and legal parentage in ART cases:

1. Intended Parents: In most cases, the intended parents, who are the individuals or couples seeking to have a child through ART, are considered the legal parents of the child. The intended parents may include both biological parents (if one or both provide the egg or sperm) or adoptive parents (if they are using a gestational surrogate or a donated embryo).

2. Gestational Surrogacy: In gestational surrogacy, the surrogate carries the child but is not biologically related to the child. The intended parents are typically recognized as the legal parents from birth or through a parentage order after birth. In some jurisdictions, pre-birth orders are granted to establish the intended parents' legal parentage before the child's birth.

3. Traditional Surrogacy: In traditional surrogacy, the surrogate provides the egg, making her the biological mother of the child. Legal arrangements for traditional surrogacy can be more complex, and parental rights may need to be established through adoption or other legal means.

4. Egg and Sperm Donation: When using donor eggs or

sperm, the intended parents are usually considered the legal parents of the child, even if they have no genetic relationship to the child.

5. Donor Agreements: In some cases, intended parents and donors may have legal agreements defining their rights and responsibilities. These agreements may address issues such as parental rights, financial arrangements, and confidentiality.

6. Birth Certificates: The birth certificate of a child conceived through ART may list the intended parents as the legal parents, even if they are not biologically related to the child. In some cases, parentage orders or other legal processes may be required to establish parental rights and amend the birth certificate.

7. Adoption: In some jurisdictions, intended parents using a surrogate or donated embryo may need to go through an adoption process to legally establish their parental rights.

8. Same-Sex Couples: The legal recognition of same-sex marriages or partnerships can also impact parental rights and legal parentage in ART cases. In many jurisdictions, same-sex couples have the same legal rights as opposite-sex couples in regard to parenting through ART.

It is crucial for individuals and couples considering ART to seek legal advice to understand the specific laws and regulations governing parental rights and legal parentage in their jurisdiction. The legal process can vary significantly depending on the location and the specific circumstances, so having proper legal guidance is essential to protect the rights and interests of all parties involved.

Domestic Violence and Family Law

Domestic violence is a serious issue that can have profound effects on individuals and families. In the context of family law, domestic violence can impact various aspects of a family's legal matters. Here are some key points regarding domestic violence and family law:

1. Protection Orders: Courts can issue protection orders (restraining orders) to protect individuals who are victims of domestic violence. These orders may prohibit the abuser from contacting, harassing, or coming near the victim and other family members. Protection orders aim to ensure the safety and well-being of those affected by domestic violence.

2. Child Custody and Visitation: Domestic violence can significantly influence child custody and visitation arrangements. Courts prioritize the best interests of the child when making decisions about custody and visitation. A history of domestic violence may impact the court's determination of custody, and arrangements may be modified to protect the child and the victim.

3. Parental Rights: In some cases, domestic violence can lead to the termination or restriction of parental rights. Courts may consider the safety and well-being of the child when making decisions about parental rights in cases involving domestic violence.

4. Divorce and Separation: Domestic violence can be a factor in divorce or separation proceedings. It may impact issues related to property division, spousal

support, and child support. Courts may consider the impact of domestic violence when making decisions about financial matters in divorce cases.

5. Mediation and Alternative Dispute Resolution: In some jurisdictions, mediation or alternative dispute resolution processes may be utilized to resolve family law issues. However, in cases involving domestic violence, mediation may not be appropriate or safe. Courts may exempt parties from mediation if there is a history of domestic violence.

6. Evidence and Documentation: Victims of domestic violence should document incidents of abuse, such as photographs, medical reports, or witness statements, as evidence for legal proceedings. This documentation can support the victim's case when seeking protection orders or other legal remedies.

7. Legal Assistance: Individuals affected by domestic violence should seek legal assistance from experienced family law attorneys or domestic violence advocates. An attorney can help victims understand their rights, guide them through the legal process, and advocate for their safety and well-being.

8. Child Protective Services: In cases where children are exposed to domestic violence, Child Protective Services (CPS) or equivalent agencies may become involved to ensure the safety and welfare of the child.

It is crucial to take domestic violence seriously and seek help from law enforcement, support services, and legal professionals. Family law courts aim to protect victims of domestic violence and promote the well-being of all family members involved. If you or someone you know is experiencing domestic violence, reach out to local resources, hotlines, or law enforcement for immediate support and assistance.

Legal protections for victims of domestic violence

Legal protections for victims of domestic violence can vary depending on the jurisdiction, but some common measures include:

1. Protection Orders: Also known as restraining orders or orders of protection, these court-issued orders prohibit the abuser from contacting, harassing, or coming near the victim and other family members. Violation of a protection order can result in criminal charges.

2. Emergency Protective Orders: In cases of immediate danger, law enforcement officers or judges can issue emergency protective orders, providing immediate protection until a formal protection order can be obtained.

3. Mandatory Arrest Policies: Some jurisdictions have mandatory arrest policies, requiring law enforcement officers to make an arrest if they have probable cause to believe that domestic violence has occurred.

4. Confidentiality: Courts may keep the victim's address and contact information confidential to prevent the abuser from locating them.

5. Custody and Visitation Modifications: In cases of domestic violence, custody and visitation arrangements may be modified to ensure the safety and well-being of the children involved.

6. Housing Protections: Some jurisdictions provide

housing protections for victims of domestic violence, such as the ability to break a lease without penalty or eviction protection.

7. Immigration Protections: Victims of domestic violence who are undocumented immigrants may be eligible for certain immigration protections, such as a U visa or a Violence Against Women Act (VAWA) self-petition.

8. Employment Protections: Some jurisdictions have laws that protect victims of domestic violence from employment discrimination or allow them to take time off from work to address domestic violence-related issues.

9. Confidentiality in Court Proceedings: In some cases, court proceedings related to domestic violence may be closed to the public to protect the victim's privacy and safety.

10. Gun Restrictions: In some jurisdictions, individuals subject to protection orders may be prohibited from possessing firearms.

It is important to note that laws and legal protections may differ depending on the location. Victims of domestic violence should seek help from local resources, domestic violence hotlines, law enforcement, and legal professionals to understand their rights and the available legal protections. If you or someone you know is experiencing domestic violence, reaching out for support and assistance can be critical for safety and well-being.

Restraining orders and protective orders

Restraining orders and protective orders are legal measures that aim to protect individuals from harm or harassment, especially in cases of domestic violence or abuse. While the specific terminology and details may vary depending on the jurisdiction, the general concepts are as follows:

1. Restraining Order: A restraining order is a court-issued order that prohibits one person from contacting or coming near another person. It is typically requested by a victim who feels threatened or unsafe due to the actions of another individual. Restraining orders can be temporary or permanent and may include provisions for keeping a certain distance from the protected person, refraining from contacting them or their family members, and avoiding places where the protected person may be present. Violation of a restraining order can lead to legal consequences, including fines and imprisonment.

2. Protective Order: A protective order is similar to a restraining order and is also issued by the court to protect a victim from harm or harassment. Protective orders may be broader in scope and can cover situations beyond domestic violence, such as harassment, stalking, or elder abuse. Like restraining orders, protective orders may have specific provisions to keep the protected person safe and may involve penalties for violations.

It is important to note that the terminology and procedures for obtaining restraining or protective orders may differ based on the jurisdiction. In some places, the terms "restraining order" and "protective order" may be used interchangeably, while in others, they may have distinct legal meanings.

If someone is facing threats or harassment and believes they need protection, they should reach out to their local law enforcement or seek legal advice to understand the available options for obtaining a restraining or protective order. These legal measures can provide critical support and safety for individuals who are experiencing harmful situations.

Impact of domestic violence on child custody and visitation

Domestic violence can have significant implications on child custody and visitation decisions during divorce or separation proceedings. The impact varies depending on the specific circumstances and the severity of the domestic violence, but here are some general considerations:

1. Child Safety: The court's primary concern in child custody cases is the best interests of the child. If there is evidence of domestic violence and it is determined to pose a risk to the child's safety, the court may prioritize the safety of the child and limit the abusive parent's access or even deny them custody altogether.

2. Parental Fitness: Domestic violence can call into question the fitness of the abusive parent to care for the child. The court will assess the ability of each parent to provide a safe and stable environment for the child. Evidence of domestic violence may lead to supervised visitation or restricted contact with the child.

3. Protective Orders: If there is a history of domestic violence, the court may issue protective orders to protect the child and the non-abusive parent. These orders can restrict the abusive parent's contact with the child or require supervised visitation until the court is satisfied that the child's safety is not at risk.

4. Custody Evaluations: In some cases, the court may order custody evaluations conducted by mental health

professionals to assess the fitness of both parents and the impact of domestic violence on the child.

5. Evidence and Documentation: Documentation of domestic violence, such as police reports, medical records, or witness statements, can be crucial in presenting the case to the court. Providing evidence of domestic violence can strengthen the argument for protecting the child's well-being.

It is essential for anyone facing domestic violence concerns in a child custody or visitation dispute to seek legal advice from an experienced family law attorney. Each case is unique, and an attorney can help navigate the legal process and advocate for the best interests of the child.

Family Dispute Resolution

Family Dispute Resolution (FDR) is a process designed to help families and individuals resolve conflicts and disagreements outside of court. It is particularly relevant in family law cases, such as divorce, child custody, and property division disputes. The primary goal of FDR is to facilitate open communication and negotiation to reach mutually acceptable solutions.

Key aspects of Family Dispute Resolution include:

1. Mediation: Mediation is a common form of FDR where a neutral third party, known as a mediator, helps the parties in dispute communicate effectively, identify their interests and needs, and explore potential solutions. The mediator does not make decisions but assists in facilitating a voluntary agreement.

2. Collaborative Law: In collaborative law, each party is represented by their respective attorneys, and all commit to resolving the issues through negotiation rather than litigation. Collaborative law encourages a cooperative and respectful approach to resolving conflicts.

3. Family Counseling: FDR may involve family counseling or therapy, especially in cases involving children. Family counselors can help families address emotional and relationship issues and find constructive ways to resolve disputes.

4. Parenting Plans: In child custody cases, FDR focuses on developing parenting plans that address the needs and best interests of the child. These plans outline the time-sharing arrangements, decision-making

responsibilities, and communication between parents.

5. Financial Agreements: FDR can also help parties in a divorce or separation reach agreements on property division, spousal support, and child support, taking into account the financial needs and circumstances of each party.

Benefits of Family Dispute Resolution:

- Confidentiality: FDR provides a private and confidential environment for discussing sensitive family matters.
- Cost-Effective: Compared to litigation, FDR is often more cost-effective as it can avoid expensive court proceedings.
- Empowerment: FDR empowers individuals to participate actively in the decision-making process and find solutions that work best for their unique circumstances.
- Preservation of Relationships: By promoting open communication and cooperation, FDR can help preserve family relationships, especially when children are involved.

Family Dispute Resolution is not suitable for all situations, especially in cases involving abuse, violence, or situations where power imbalances exist. In such instances, the safety and well-being of the parties may necessitate a different approach, such as court intervention.

Overall, Family Dispute Resolution provides families with a constructive and collaborative alternative to resolving conflicts, fostering healthier outcomes and paving the way for a more stable future.

Mediation and alternative dispute resolution in family law

Mediation and alternative dispute resolution (ADR) play a crucial role in family law cases, offering parties an opportunity to resolve their issues outside of court through facilitated negotiation. These processes aim to promote cooperation, communication, and understanding between the parties involved, resulting in mutually acceptable agreements that serve the best interests of the family members, especially children.

Key features of mediation and ADR in family law include:

1. Mediation: Mediation is a voluntary and confidential process in which a neutral third party, known as a mediator, assists the parties in identifying their needs, interests, and concerns. The mediator facilitates communication and guides the parties towards finding solutions to their disputes. The goal is to reach a mutually acceptable agreement on issues such as child custody, visitation, support, and property division.

2. Collaborative Law: Collaborative law is an ADR process where both parties, along with their respective attorneys, commit to resolving the issues through negotiation and cooperation. The collaborative approach fosters a team-oriented atmosphere and encourages open communication to reach fair and lasting agreements.

3. Arbitration: While less common in family law, arbitration involves the appointment of a neutral arbitrator who acts as a private judge to make decisions on contested issues. The parties agree to abide by the arbitrator's decision, and the process can be less formal and time-consuming than traditional court proceedings.

4. Parenting Coordination: Parenting coordination is a specialized ADR process designed to assist high-conflict co-parents in resolving ongoing parenting disputes. A parenting coordinator, often a mental health professional or attorney, helps facilitate communication, implement parenting plans, and make recommendations to the court when necessary.

Benefits of Mediation and ADR in Family Law:

- Empowerment: Mediation and ADR give parties more control over the outcome of their case, empowering them to actively participate in the decision-making process.
- Preservation of Relationships: These processes foster a more amicable environment for resolving disputes, promoting healthier co-parenting relationships and reducing the negative impact of conflict on children.
- Cost-Effectiveness: Mediation and ADR are generally less expensive than going to court, saving parties time and money.
- Privacy: These processes are confidential, offering a secure setting for discussing personal and sensitive family matters.

While mediation and ADR can be effective in many family law cases, they may not be suitable for situations involving domestic violence, abuse, or significant power imbalances. In such instances, court intervention and protective measures may be necessary to ensure the safety and well-being of all involved parties.

In conclusion, mediation and alternative dispute resolution provide families with constructive and collaborative options for resolving their issues, promoting cooperation, and supporting the overall well-being of family members.

Collaborative law and its benefits

Collaborative law is a unique approach to dispute resolution that focuses on fostering cooperation and open communication between the parties involved. It is particularly prevalent in family law cases, such as divorce and child custody disputes, but can also be utilized in other civil matters. The key features and benefits of collaborative law include:

1. Voluntary Process: Collaborative law is a voluntary process, meaning that all parties involved must willingly commit to resolving their issues through collaboration and negotiation. This commitment sets the foundation for a more cooperative and productive atmosphere.
2. Focus on Interests and Needs: In collaborative law, the focus shifts from positions and demands to the underlying interests and needs of each party. This helps to uncover the root causes of disputes and allows for the exploration of creative solutions that address the specific concerns of all involved.
3. Team-Oriented Approach: Collaborative law embraces a team-oriented approach, involving the parties, their respective attorneys, and often other professionals, such as financial experts, mental health professionals, or child specialists. This multi-disciplinary team works together to find comprehensive solutions that consider all aspects of the case.
4. Open Communication: A hallmark of collaborative law is its emphasis on open and transparent communication. Parties are encouraged to express

their feelings and concerns in a safe and respectful environment, leading to better understanding and more effective problem-solving.

5. Confidentiality: Collaborative law proceedings are confidential, which means that discussions and negotiations that take place within the process remain private. This can create a more comfortable space for the parties to share information and make informed decisions without fear of public exposure.

6. Cost-Effectiveness: Compared to traditional litigation, collaborative law can be more cost-effective. The focus on cooperation and efficiency can lead to a quicker resolution, reducing the overall expenses associated with lengthy court proceedings.

7. Preserving Relationships: Collaborative law is especially beneficial in family law cases, where preserving relationships, particularly those involving co-parenting, is essential. The collaborative approach aims to minimize conflict and help parties maintain respectful and amicable interactions.

8. Tailored Solutions: Collaborative law allows parties to create customized solutions that suit their unique circumstances and meet their specific needs. This level of personalization can lead to more satisfying and sustainable agreements.

9. Avoiding Courtroom Battles: By engaging in collaborative law, parties can avoid the adversarial nature of court proceedings, which can be emotionally draining and can strain relationships further.

10. Emphasis on the Future: Collaborative law encourages parties to focus on their future rather than dwelling on past grievances. This forward-thinking approach can lead to more positive outcomes and a smoother transition to the next phase of life.

Collaborative law is not suitable for all cases, particularly those involving domestic violence, extreme power imbalances, or situations where parties are unwilling to cooperate. However, when parties are committed to finding mutually beneficial solutions and are open to a cooperative process, collaborative law can be an effective and rewarding method of resolving disputes.

Litigation and court proceedings in family disputes

Litigation and court proceedings play a crucial role in resolving family disputes when other methods, such as mediation or collaborative law, are not feasible or unsuccessful. Family law litigation involves taking legal issues to court to be decided by a judge or jury. While litigation is sometimes perceived as an adversarial and contentious process, it remains an essential option for protecting individuals' rights and ensuring fair resolutions. Here's an overview of how litigation and court proceedings work in family disputes:

1. Filing a Petition: The litigation process begins with one party filing a petition or complaint with the court, outlining the legal issues at hand, such as divorce, child custody, child support, alimony, or property division.

2. Response and Counterclaims: The other party then has the opportunity to respond to the petition and may file counterclaims if they have additional issues they wish to address.

3. Discovery: During the discovery phase, both parties exchange information, documents, and evidence relevant to the case. Discovery may include requests for documents, interrogatories (written questions), depositions (oral testimonies under oath), and expert evaluations.

4. Pre-Trial Motions: Before the trial, either party may file pre-trial motions to address specific legal issues

or request certain actions by the court. Common pre-trial motions include motions for temporary orders or motions to dismiss parts of the case.

5. Settlement Negotiations: Even in the midst of litigation, parties may engage in settlement negotiations with the guidance of their attorneys to reach an agreement outside of court. Settlements can save time, money, and emotional stress for all involved.

6. Trial: If a settlement cannot be reached, the case proceeds to trial. During the trial, each party presents evidence, witnesses, and arguments to support their position. The judge or jury then makes decisions on the disputed issues based on the presented evidence and applicable laws.

7. Court Orders: Once the trial concludes, the court issues orders that legally resolve the matters at hand. These orders may address child custody and visitation schedules, child support, alimony, property division, and other relevant issues.

8. Post-Trial Motions: After the trial, either party may file post-trial motions, such as motions for reconsideration or appeals, if they believe there were errors in the court's decision.

9. Enforcement and Modification: Once court orders are in place, parties are legally obligated to follow them. If one party fails to comply with the court's orders, the other party may seek enforcement through the court. Additionally, if circumstances change significantly, either party may seek modifications to existing court orders.

While family law litigation can be time-consuming, emotionally challenging, and costly, it serves as a critical tool to resolve complex and contentious family issues when alternative dispute resolution methods are not viable. An experienced family law attorney can guide individuals through the litigation process, provide legal counsel, and work to protect their rights and interests during these difficult times.

International Family Law

International family law involves legal issues and disputes that cross international borders and impact families with connections to different countries. It deals with complex and diverse matters related to marriage, divorce, child custody, child abduction, adoption, and property rights, among others, where multiple jurisdictions and legal systems may be involved. Here's an overview of some key aspects of international family law:

1. Jurisdiction: One of the primary challenges in international family law is determining which country's laws and courts have jurisdiction over a particular case. Jurisdictional issues can arise in cases of divorce, child custody, and property division when spouses or parents have connections to different countries.

2. Child Custody and International Abduction: International child custody disputes can arise when one parent takes a child to another country without the other parent's consent or fails to return the child after a visitation period. The Hague Convention on the Civil Aspects of International Child Abduction is an international treaty designed to facilitate the prompt return of abducted children to their country of habitual residence.

3. International Adoption: Adopting a child from another country involves navigating the legal requirements of both the child's country of origin and the adoptive parents' home country. International adoption laws vary widely, and it is essential to ensure

compliance with all relevant regulations.

4. Marriage and Divorce: Marriages involving spouses from different countries may present complex legal issues regarding the validity of the marriage, property division, and jurisdiction for divorce proceedings.
5. Prenuptial and Postnuptial Agreements: Couples with international connections may opt for prenuptial or postnuptial agreements to address potential legal issues related to property rights and financial matters in the event of divorce.
6. Property Division: Dividing assets and property in international divorces can be particularly challenging, especially when the assets are located in different countries or subject to different legal systems.
7. International Child Support: Determining child support obligations when parents reside in different countries involves understanding the applicable laws and mechanisms for enforcement.
8. Cultural Considerations: International family law also requires sensitivity to cultural differences and norms, as well as an understanding of how these may intersect with legal issues.
9. Enforcement of Foreign Judgments: Enforcing court orders from one country in another can be complicated, and international treaties and agreements may govern the recognition and enforcement of foreign judgments.

Navigating international family law issues requires a thorough understanding of both domestic and international laws, as well as the ability to work across legal systems and cultural boundaries. Parties involved in international family law matters often seek the assistance of experienced family law attorneys with expertise in handling cases with international dimensions to protect their rights and interests effectively.

Cross-border family law issues and jurisdiction

Cross-border family law issues and jurisdiction are complex and challenging legal matters that arise when a family's connections span multiple countries. Determining which country's laws and courts have authority to handle a particular case can significantly impact the outcome and rights of the parties involved. Here are some key aspects of cross-border family law issues and jurisdiction:

1. Habitual Residence: The concept of habitual residence is central in cross-border family law cases involving child custody and abduction. It refers to the country where a child has lived with a sense of continuity and stability. Determining a child's habitual residence is crucial in cases of international child custody disputes and abduction, as it determines which country's courts have jurisdiction.

2. Forum Shopping: Forum shopping occurs when one party seeks to initiate legal proceedings in a specific country or jurisdiction that may be more favorable to their case. It can lead to jurisdictional disputes and complicates the resolution of cross-border family law matters.

3. The Hague Conventions: The Hague Conventions are a series of international treaties designed to address specific cross-border family law issues. For example, The Hague Convention on the Civil Aspects of International Child Abduction deals with the prompt

return of abducted children to their country of habitual residence.

4. Divorce Jurisdiction: In cases of international divorce, determining the appropriate jurisdiction for divorce proceedings can be challenging. Parties may have connections to different countries, and the laws of each jurisdiction may affect issues like property division, spousal support, and child custody.

5. Recognition and Enforcement of Foreign Judgments: Enforcing court orders and judgments from one country in another requires an understanding of international law and treaties. Some countries may recognize and enforce foreign judgments under specific conditions, while others may not.

6. Conflicting Laws: Cross-border family law issues can involve conflicting laws from different jurisdictions. This can complicate matters such as property division, child custody, and child support, requiring legal professionals to navigate complex legal landscapes.

7. Cultural Sensitivity: Cultural differences can significantly impact cross-border family law cases. Understanding and respecting cultural norms and practices is essential when dealing with international family matters.

8. International Child Support: Determining child support obligations when parents reside in different countries involves understanding the applicable laws and mechanisms for enforcement.

9. Language and Translation: Language barriers and translation issues may arise in cross-border family law cases, making effective communication and legal representation more challenging.

Navigating cross-border family law issues and jurisdiction requires specialized knowledge of both domestic and international laws, as well as the ability to work across legal systems and cultural boundaries. Parties involved in such cases often seek the assistance of experienced family law attorneys with expertise in international matters to ensure their rights are protected and that legal proceedings are conducted appropriately across borders.

International child abduction and the Hague Convention

International child abduction refers to the wrongful removal or retention of a child from their country of habitual residence by one parent without the consent of the other parent or legal guardian. This act can disrupt the child's life and custody arrangements, leading to emotional distress and legal challenges for both parents.

To address this issue and protect the rights of children and parents involved, the international community established The Hague Convention on the Civil Aspects of International Child Abduction, commonly known as the Hague Abduction Convention. The convention was adopted in 1980 and has been ratified by over 100 countries.

Key provisions of the Hague Abduction Convention include:

1. Return of the Child: The primary goal of the convention is to ensure the prompt return of an abducted child to their country of habitual residence, where custody issues can be decided by the appropriate authorities.

2. Habitual Residence: The convention defines "habitual residence" as the country where a child has lived with a sense of continuity and stability before the abduction occurred. Determining the habitual residence is crucial in deciding which country's courts have jurisdiction over the custody dispute.

3. Rights of Custody: The convention defines "rights of

custody" as the rights and responsibilities that parents or guardians have in making decisions concerning the child's upbringing, including issues related to education, religion, and healthcare.

4. Central Authorities: Each member country designates a Central Authority responsible for facilitating communication and cooperation between countries in cases of child abduction. The Central Authorities work together to locate abducted children, initiate legal proceedings, and enforce court orders for the child's return.

5. Limited Defenses: The Hague Abduction Convention provides limited defenses to the return of a child, such as the risk of physical or psychological harm to the child or if the child has reached an age and level of maturity where their objections to the return are considered.

6. Expedited Proceedings: The convention requires that legal proceedings for the return of an abducted child be conducted expeditiously to minimize the time the child spends away from their habitual residence.

While the Hague Abduction Convention is a critical tool in resolving international child abduction cases, its effectiveness depends on the cooperation between member countries and their commitment to upholding its principles. Some challenges may arise due to differences in legal systems, language barriers, and cultural norms.

Families dealing with international child abduction cases are advised to seek legal assistance from experienced family law attorneys with expertise in international matters. These professionals can guide parents through the process of filing a Hague Convention application and representing their interests in both their home country and the country where the child was wrongfully taken or retained.

Recognition of foreign marriages and divorces

Recognition of foreign marriages and divorces refers to the legal acknowledgment and acceptance of marital status and dissolution of marriage obtained in a foreign country by a country's legal system. It is an essential aspect of international family law, ensuring consistency and validity of marital and divorce status across different jurisdictions.

The recognition of foreign marriages typically involves the following considerations:

1. Legal Capacity: For a foreign marriage to be recognized, both parties must have had the legal capacity to marry under the laws of the country where the marriage took place and the laws of the country where recognition is sought.

2. Formal Requirements: The marriage must have been conducted according to the formal requirements of the foreign country, such as obtaining the necessary documentation, solemnization, and registration.

3. Consistency with Public Policy: The foreign marriage must not contravene the public policy of the country where recognition is sought. For example, marriages involving minors or polygamous marriages may not be recognized in some jurisdictions.

4. Marriage Validity: The marriage must be valid in the country where it took place. If the marriage would be considered void or invalid in the foreign country, it is

unlikely to be recognized elsewhere.

On the other hand, the recognition of foreign divorces involves:

1. Jurisdiction: The court that granted the divorce must have had proper jurisdiction over the matter. This includes jurisdiction over the parties involved and the authority to hear divorce cases.
2. Notice and Due Process: Both parties must have received proper notice of the divorce proceedings, and due process must have been followed.
3. Compliance with Foreign Laws: The divorce must have been granted in accordance with the laws of the foreign country.
4. Consistency with Public Policy: The terms and conditions of the divorce should not violate the public policy of the country where recognition is sought.

The rules and procedures for recognizing foreign marriages and divorces can vary significantly from one country to another. Some countries have specific laws or conventions that govern the recognition of foreign family law matters, while others may have common law principles or international agreements in place.

It is essential for individuals seeking recognition of their foreign marriages or divorces to seek legal advice and assistance from qualified family law attorneys who specialize in international family law. These professionals can guide them through the complex legal processes and ensure that their marital status or divorce is appropriately recognized in the desired jurisdiction.

Family Law and Child Welfare

Family law and child welfare are closely interconnected areas of law that focus on the well-being and protection of children within the family unit. Family law deals with legal issues related to marriage, divorce, custody, and support, while child welfare focuses on safeguarding the welfare and rights of children who may be at risk of abuse, neglect, or other forms of harm.

Key aspects of the relationship between family law and child welfare include:

1. Child Custody and Visitation: Family courts decide child custody and visitation arrangements during divorce or separation proceedings. The court considers the best interests of the child when determining custody and visitation, ensuring that the child's physical and emotional needs are met.

2. Child Support: Family law also addresses child support, where one parent may be required to financially support the child after divorce or separation. Ensuring adequate financial support contributes to the child's well-being.

3. Child Protection: Child welfare agencies, such as child protective services, work to protect children from abuse, neglect, or unsafe living conditions. If there are concerns about a child's safety, these agencies may intervene to assess the situation and take necessary actions to protect the child.

4. Foster Care and Adoption: Child welfare agencies may place children in foster care when they are unable to remain with their birth families due to safety

concerns. Adoption is also a significant aspect of child welfare, providing permanent homes for children in need of stable families.

5. Juvenile Dependency Proceedings: In cases where a child is at risk of harm or is already suffering abuse or neglect, the court may initiate juvenile dependency proceedings. These proceedings focus on the child's safety and well-being, and the court may remove the child from the home temporarily or permanently if necessary.

6. Termination of Parental Rights: In severe cases of abuse or neglect, parental rights may be terminated, allowing the child to be adopted by a new family or placed in permanent care.

7. Guardianship: Family law also addresses legal guardianship, where a guardian is appointed to care for a child in cases where the parents are unable to do so.

Overall, the intersection of family law and child welfare aims to protect children's rights, ensure their safety and well-being, and create a supportive and stable environment for their growth and development. Legal professionals, social workers, and other professionals work collaboratively to safeguard the best interests of children involved in family law matters.

Child protection services and legal interventions

Child protection services and legal interventions play a crucial role in safeguarding the welfare of children who may be at risk of abuse, neglect, or harm. These services are typically provided by government agencies at the state or local level and are designed to ensure the safety and well-being of children.

Child protection services and legal interventions involve the following key components:

1. Reporting and Investigation: Anyone who suspects that a child is being abused or neglected can make a report to the child protection agency. Upon receiving a report, the agency initiates an investigation to assess the child's safety and the allegations made in the report. This may involve interviews with the child, family members, and other individuals involved in the child's life.

2. Emergency Removal: In cases where the child is in immediate danger, child protection services may take emergency action to remove the child from the home. This ensures the child's safety while the investigation is ongoing.

3. Assessing Safety and Risk: Child protection agencies conduct assessments to determine the level of risk to the child's safety. Based on the assessment, they may develop a safety plan to address any immediate dangers.

4. Family Preservation: Child protection services aim to support families in addressing the issues that led to the report of abuse or neglect. Family preservation services may include counseling, parenting classes, and other support to help families create a safe environment for their children.

5. Court Involvement: In some cases, legal interventions are necessary to protect the child's well-being. Child protection agencies may file a petition in family court seeking temporary or permanent custody of the child, termination of parental rights, or other legal measures to ensure the child's safety.

6. Foster Care: If it is not safe for the child to remain in the home, child protection services may place the child in foster care with a temporary caregiver. Foster care provides a stable and nurturing environment for the child while family issues are addressed.

7. Reunification or Adoption: The ultimate goal of child protection services is to ensure the child's safety and well-being. Depending on the circumstances, the child may be reunified with the birth family once safety concerns are resolved, or the child may be placed for adoption if reunification is not possible.

Child protection services work collaboratively with law enforcement, social workers, healthcare professionals, and other stakeholders to protect vulnerable children and promote their best interests. Legal interventions, when necessary, are guided by state laws and regulations, and decisions are made in family court to ensure the child's safety and long-term well-being.

Foster care and kinship care arrangements

Foster care and kinship care are two types of out-of-home care arrangements for children who cannot live safely with their birth families. These arrangements are designed to provide a temporary or permanent living situation that ensures the child's safety, well-being, and development.

1. Foster Care:
    - Foster care is a temporary placement option for children who are unable to live with their birth parents due to abuse, neglect, or other safety concerns.
    - Foster parents are trained and licensed caregivers who provide a stable and nurturing home for the child while the family issues are addressed.
    - Foster care is intended to be a temporary solution, and the goal is usually to reunify the child with their birth family once safety concerns are resolved.
    - Foster parents play a crucial role in supporting the child's emotional, educational, and physical needs during their time in care.
    - Foster care agencies and social workers closely monitor the child's progress and work with the birth family to address the issues that led to the child's placement.
2. Kinship Care:
    - Kinship care is a placement option where a

child is placed with a relative or someone with a significant relationship to the child, such as a grandparent, aunt, uncle, or close family friend.

- Kinship care is considered a preferred option when a child cannot live with their birth parents because it maintains the child's connection to their family and community.
- Kinship caregivers often have a pre-existing relationship with the child, which can provide a sense of familiarity and stability during a challenging time.
- Like foster parents, kinship caregivers also receive support and services to meet the child's needs and ensure a safe and nurturing environment.

Key aspects of both foster care and kinship care arrangements include:

- Regular assessments of the child's well-being and safety in the placement.
- Collaboration with child welfare agencies, social workers, and other professionals to support the child and caregivers.
- Access to services and resources to meet the child's physical, emotional, educational, and health needs.
- Efforts to maintain the child's connections to their birth family, culture, and community whenever possible.
- Ongoing efforts to address the family's issues and reunify the child with their birth family, if appropriate and safe.

Both foster care and kinship care aim to provide stable and loving homes for children during challenging times and support their growth and development. These care arrangements can have a significant impact on a child's life, and the caregivers' commitment and dedication play a crucial role in promoting the child's well-being and long-term success.

Termination of parental rights and adoption

Termination of parental rights and adoption are legal processes that can significantly impact the lives of children and families. These processes are typically pursued when it is deemed in the best interest of the child to have a stable and permanent home with new caregivers.

1. Termination of Parental Rights (TPR):
    - Termination of parental rights is a legal process through which a parent's legal rights and responsibilities to their child are permanently severed.
    - TPR is typically pursued when a parent has demonstrated ongoing and significant neglect, abuse, or inability to care for the child.
    - The court may consider TPR if the parent has a history of substance abuse, chronic neglect, abandonment, or has engaged in conduct that endangers the child's well-being.
    - The process involves a court hearing where evidence is presented to demonstrate the need for TPR, and the court makes a determination based on the child's best interests.
    - Termination of parental rights is a serious step, and it is meant to provide the child with a more stable and secure home environment.

2. Adoption:
    - Adoption is a legal process through which

a child becomes a permanent member of a new family, and the adoptive parents assume all the legal rights and responsibilities of the child's birth parents.

- Adoption is often pursued after TPR has been granted, or in cases where a child is already legally free for adoption, such as in cases of relinquishment or abandonment.
- Adoptive parents go through a rigorous screening and assessment process to ensure they can provide a stable and loving home for the child.
- The court oversees the adoption process to ensure that it is in the child's best interests and that all legal requirements are met.
- Adoption grants the child the same legal rights and protections as if they were born into the adoptive family.

It's essential to note that termination of parental rights is a complex and emotional process, and it is generally considered a last resort when all efforts to reunify the child with their birth family have been unsuccessful or deemed unsafe. The focus of both TPR and adoption is to prioritize the well-being and best interests of the child, ensuring they have the opportunity for a loving and stable home environment.

Adoption can be a life-changing experience for both the child and the adoptive family, providing them with the opportunity to build a lifelong bond and create a new and loving family unit. It is a legal and emotional process that requires careful consideration and commitment from all parties involved.

Family Law and Elder Care

Family Law and Elder Care address legal issues and considerations that arise when caring for elderly family members. As individuals age, their needs may change, and families often face complex decisions related to their well-being, healthcare, and financial affairs. Family law plays a crucial role in providing legal frameworks to protect the rights and interests of elderly individuals and their families.

1. Guardianship and Conservatorship:
   - Guardianship and conservatorship are legal arrangements that allow a designated individual or entity to make decisions on behalf of an elderly person who is no longer able to manage their personal and financial affairs due to incapacity.
   - Guardianship focuses on personal matters, such as healthcare decisions and living arrangements, while conservatorship involves managing the individual's finances and assets.
   - The process involves filing a petition with the court to determine the elderly person's capacity and appoint a suitable guardian or conservator if necessary.
2. Healthcare Directives and Power of Attorney:
   - Healthcare directives, such as living wills and durable power of attorney for healthcare, allow individuals to express their preferences regarding medical treatment and end-of-life

care.

- Power of attorney enables a designated person (the agent) to make healthcare decisions on behalf of the elderly individual if they are unable to do so.

3. Long-Term Care Planning:

- Long-term care planning involves creating a comprehensive strategy to address the financial and healthcare needs of elderly family members as they age.
- This may include exploring options for assisted living, nursing homes, or in-home care, and considering how to finance these services, such as through long-term care insurance or Medicaid.

4. Elder Abuse and Protection:

- Family law also plays a role in protecting elderly individuals from abuse and exploitation.
- Legal measures can be taken to address instances of physical, emotional, or financial abuse, neglect, or undue influence.

5. Estate Planning:

- Estate planning is essential for elderly individuals to ensure their assets are distributed according to their wishes after their passing.
- This may involve creating wills, trusts, and other legal instruments to manage their estate.

6. Family Dynamics and Dispute Resolution:

- Family law practitioners can assist in resolving conflicts that may arise among family members regarding elder care and estate matters.
- Mediation or other forms of alternative

dispute resolution can help families find amicable solutions.

Elder care is a sensitive and complex area, and family law provides the legal framework to protect the rights and well-being of elderly individuals and their families. It involves a compassionate and holistic approach to addressing the evolving needs of aging family members and ensuring their dignity, autonomy, and safety.

Legal issues in elder care and guardianship

Legal issues in elder care and guardianship are crucial aspects of family law that revolve around protecting the rights and well-being of elderly individuals who may face challenges in managing their personal and financial affairs due to incapacity or vulnerability. These issues often arise when elderly individuals require assistance with decision-making and care, and they can involve complex legal processes. Some key legal issues in elder care and guardianship include:

1. Capacity Assessment: Determining an elderly person's capacity to make decisions is fundamental in elder care and guardianship cases. Medical and legal professionals may conduct capacity assessments to evaluate an individual's ability to understand and make informed choices about their healthcare, finances, and daily living.

2. Guardianship and Conservatorship: When an elderly individual is deemed incapacitated and unable to manage their affairs, a guardianship or conservatorship may be necessary. A guardian is appointed to make personal decisions on behalf of the elderly person, such as healthcare and living arrangements. A conservator is responsible for managing the elderly person's financial affairs.

3. Healthcare Directives: Healthcare directives, such as living wills and durable powers of attorney for healthcare, allow elderly individuals to express their preferences regarding medical treatment and end-of-life care. These legal documents ensure that their

healthcare decisions align with their wishes.

4. Financial Abuse and Exploitation: Elderly individuals are vulnerable to financial abuse and exploitation. Family law addresses legal measures to protect elderly individuals from financial scams, undue influence, and other forms of exploitation.

5. Long-Term Care Planning: Long-term care planning involves developing a comprehensive strategy to address the financial and healthcare needs of elderly individuals as they age. This may include exploring options for assisted living, nursing homes, or in-home care, and determining how to finance these services.

6. Elder Abuse: Family law addresses issues related to elder abuse, which can be physical, emotional, or financial in nature. Legal measures can be taken to protect elderly individuals from abuse and neglect.

7. Estate Planning: Estate planning is essential for elderly individuals to ensure their assets are distributed according to their wishes after their passing. This may involve creating wills, trusts, and other legal instruments to manage their estate.

8. Dispute Resolution: Family law practitioners may assist in resolving conflicts that may arise among family members regarding elder care and guardianship matters. Mediation or other forms of alternative dispute resolution can help families find solutions that are in the best interests of the elderly individual.

Elder care and guardianship issues require a compassionate and thoughtful approach, considering the unique needs and circumstances of elderly individuals. Family law provides the legal framework to safeguard the rights and dignity of elderly individuals and support their families in making decisions that promote their well-being and quality of life.

Advance directives and end-of-life decisions

Advance directives and end-of-life decisions are critical aspects of family law that pertain to an individual's wishes regarding medical treatment and care if they become unable to communicate or make decisions for themselves due to illness or incapacitation. These legal documents allow individuals to maintain control over their healthcare and ensure that their preferences are followed, even when they are unable to advocate for themselves. Some key components of advance directives and end-of-life decisions include:

1. Living Will: A living will is a legal document that outlines an individual's preferences for medical treatment in specific situations, particularly those involving life-sustaining measures. It provides guidance to healthcare professionals and family members on the individual's wishes if they are in a terminal condition or a persistent vegetative state and unable to communicate.

2. Durable Power of Attorney for Healthcare: This legal document designates a trusted person (healthcare proxy or agent) to make healthcare decisions on behalf of the individual if they are unable to do so. The designated person should be someone who understands the individual's values and beliefs and can advocate for their medical preferences.

3. Do Not Resuscitate (DNR) Order: A DNR order is a medical directive that instructs healthcare providers not to perform cardiopulmonary resuscitation (CPR) if the individual's heart stops or they stop breathing.

DNR orders are usually included in an individual's advance directives.

4. Medical Power of Attorney: This legal document designates a person (medical agent or surrogate) to make medical decisions on behalf of the individual, not just limited to end-of-life situations. The medical power of attorney provides broader decision-making authority for healthcare matters.

5. Hospice Care: Family law may address the option of hospice care, which focuses on providing comfort and support to individuals with terminal illnesses. Hospice care aims to improve the quality of life during the final stages of life.

6. Organ Donation: Advance directives may also address an individual's wishes regarding organ and tissue donation after their passing. This allows individuals to express their desire to contribute to saving lives through organ transplantation.

End-of-life decisions and advance directives are deeply personal choices that allow individuals to have a say in their medical care and treatment when they are unable to advocate for themselves. These documents are essential for ensuring that an individual's wishes are respected, reducing potential family conflicts, and providing peace of mind for both the individual and their loved ones. Family law provides the legal framework to ensure that advance directives are legally recognized and followed, allowing individuals to have their preferences upheld with dignity and respect.

Long-term care planning and financing

Long-term care planning and financing are critical aspects of family law that address the financial and logistical challenges associated with providing care for individuals with chronic illnesses, disabilities, or other long-term care needs. As the population ages and healthcare costs rise, long-term care planning becomes increasingly important for individuals and families to ensure quality care and financial security. Some key considerations and strategies for long-term care planning and financing include:

1. Assessment of Long-Term Care Needs: The first step in long-term care planning is to assess the individual's specific care needs. This involves evaluating their health status, medical conditions, functional abilities, and support requirements to determine the level of care needed.

2. Care Options: Long-term care can be provided in various settings, including home care, assisted living facilities, nursing homes, or adult day care centers. Each option comes with different costs and levels of support, and the choice depends on the individual's preferences and needs.

3. Medicaid Planning: Medicaid is a government program that provides financial assistance for long-term care to eligible low-income individuals. Medicaid planning involves strategies to protect assets while qualifying for Medicaid benefits, as there are income and asset limits for eligibility.

4. Long-Term Care Insurance: Long-term care insurance

is a private insurance policy that covers the costs of long-term care services. It can help individuals and families manage the financial burden of long-term care and preserve assets for other purposes.

5. Medicare Coverage: While Medicare does not typically cover long-term care in full, it may cover some aspects of skilled nursing care or short-term rehabilitation services under certain circumstances.

6. Personal Savings and Retirement Accounts: Individuals can plan for long-term care expenses by saving and investing in retirement accounts, such as IRAs and 401(k)s. Building a financial cushion can help cover future care needs.

7. Estate Planning: Estate planning, including creating wills, trusts, and durable powers of attorney, can play a significant role in long-term care planning. Proper estate planning allows individuals to designate trusted individuals to make financial and healthcare decisions on their behalf and ensure that their assets are distributed according to their wishes.

8. Reverse Mortgages: For homeowners, a reverse mortgage may be an option to tap into home equity to finance long-term care costs while still living in the home.

9. Long-Term Care Services and Supports: Exploring community-based services and support networks, such as local senior centers, caregiver support groups, and respite care, can be valuable resources for long-term care planning.

Long-term care planning is a multifaceted process that involves legal, financial, and emotional considerations. It requires open communication among family members and professional advice from attorneys, financial advisors, and elder care specialists. By proactively planning and making informed decisions, individuals and families can navigate the complexities of long-term care and ensure the best possible care and financial stability for their loved ones.

Family Law and Mental Health

Family law and mental health intersect in various ways, as mental health issues can significantly impact family dynamics, relationships, and legal proceedings. It is essential for family law professionals, such as attorneys, judges, and mediators, to have a thorough understanding of mental health issues and their implications in family law matters. Some key aspects of the relationship between family law and mental health include:

1. Child Custody and Visitation: In child custody cases, the mental health of both parents is often considered to determine the best interests of the child. Courts may assess the mental fitness of each parent and their ability to provide a safe and stable environment for the child. A parent's mental health history may influence the custody decision, and arrangements may be made to ensure the child's well-being.

2. Parental Fitness Evaluations: In some cases, courts may order parental fitness evaluations to assess the mental health and parenting capabilities of each parent involved in a custody dispute. These evaluations are conducted by mental health professionals who provide their expert opinions to the court.

3. Domestic Violence and Mental Health: Mental health issues, such as anger management problems or personality disorders, can be contributing factors in cases involving domestic violence. Understanding the mental health aspects of domestic violence is crucial in protecting victims and making appropriate legal

decisions.

4. Substance Abuse and Addiction: Substance abuse and addiction often have a profound impact on families and parenting. Family law cases involving substance abuse may require assessments, treatment recommendations, and monitoring to ensure the safety and well-being of children.

5. Guardianship and Conservatorship: Family law courts may be involved in establishing guardianship or conservatorship for individuals who are unable to manage their affairs due to mental health conditions or cognitive impairments.

6. Mental Health Treatment: Family law may intersect with mental health treatment when determining issues like the necessity of therapy or counseling for family members, especially during divorce or custody disputes.

7. Mediation and Conflict Resolution: Mental health professionals can play a crucial role in family law mediation by facilitating communication and helping parties address emotional issues constructively.

8. Parenting Plans and Co-Parenting: Mental health considerations may be essential in developing parenting plans and co-parenting arrangements to ensure the well-being of the children and support the mental health of both parents.

9. Mental Health as a Defense: In cases involving allegations of abuse or neglect, mental health issues may be raised as a defense or mitigating factor, requiring careful assessment and consideration.

10. Mental Health Advocacy: Family law attorneys may need to advocate for clients with mental health issues, ensuring their rights are protected and that they receive appropriate accommodations or support in legal proceedings.

Given the complexity and sensitivity of mental health issues in family law, it is essential for legal professionals to work collaboratively with mental health experts, such as psychologists, psychiatrists, social workers, and therapists, to make informed and compassionate decisions that promote the well-being of all family members involved. Effective collaboration between legal and mental health professionals can lead to more comprehensive and holistic solutions for families facing challenging circumstances.

Mental health considerations in family law disputes

Mental health considerations play a significant role in family law disputes and can have a profound impact on the outcome of legal proceedings. When mental health issues are present in family law cases, it is essential for all parties involved, including attorneys, judges, and mental health professionals, to approach the matter with sensitivity and expertise. Some key mental health considerations in family law disputes include:

1. Child Custody and Visitation: In child custody cases, the mental health of each parent may be evaluated to determine their ability to provide a safe and nurturing environment for the child. A parent's mental health history, current condition, and potential impact on parenting capacity are carefully assessed to ensure the child's best interests are prioritized.

2. Parental Fitness Evaluations: Courts may order parental fitness evaluations conducted by mental health professionals to assess the mental well-being and parenting capabilities of each parent involved in a custody dispute. These evaluations help provide the court with expert insights into the mental health aspects of the case.

3. Substance Abuse and Addiction: Family law cases involving substance abuse or addiction require mental health considerations, as these issues can significantly affect a person's ability to parent effectively and contribute to family stability.

4. Domestic Violence and Trauma: Mental health considerations are essential in cases involving domestic violence, as victims may experience trauma that affects their ability to navigate legal proceedings. Understanding the impact of trauma is crucial in providing appropriate support and protection for victims.

5. Mediation and Conflict Resolution: Mental health professionals can play a valuable role in family law mediation by facilitating communication and helping parties address emotional issues constructively. Mediators with a background in mental health can create a safe and supportive environment for productive discussions.

6. Child and Family Therapy: In some cases, family therapy or counseling may be recommended to address underlying mental health issues that impact family dynamics and relationships.

7. Mental Health Treatment: Family law cases may involve considerations for mental health treatment, such as therapy or counseling, to support individuals in coping with the challenges of legal disputes and family changes.

8. Parenting Plans and Co-Parenting: Mental health considerations are essential in developing parenting plans and co-parenting arrangements that promote the well-being of the children and support the mental health of both parents.

9. Capacity Assessments: In cases involving elder care or guardianship, mental health capacity assessments may be conducted to determine an individual's ability to make informed decisions.

10. Mental Health as a Defense or Mitigating Factor: In certain cases, mental health issues may be raised as a defense or mitigating factor, requiring thorough assessment and consideration of how these

conditions impact the legal matter at hand.

It is essential for legal professionals to be knowledgeable about mental health issues and their implications in family law cases. Collaborating with mental health experts, such as psychologists, psychiatrists, social workers, and therapists, can provide valuable insights and support for families facing mental health-related challenges in the legal system. By prioritizing the mental well-being of all parties involved, family law disputes can be approached with compassion and understanding, leading to more equitable and effective outcomes.

Involuntary commitment and legal rights

Involuntary commitment refers to the process of placing an individual with a mental health condition into a psychiatric hospital or mental health facility against their will. It is typically done to protect the person or others from harm when the individual is deemed to be a danger to themselves or others due to their mental health condition. Involuntary commitment laws and procedures vary by jurisdiction, but they generally involve several key aspects:

1. Criteria for Involuntary Commitment: Each jurisdiction has specific criteria that must be met for a person to be involuntarily committed. Common criteria include posing a risk of harm to oneself or others, being unable to care for oneself, or being unable to make informed decisions about treatment due to the severity of the mental health condition.

2. Evaluation and Assessment: Involuntary commitment typically begins with an evaluation by a mental health professional, often conducted in an emergency room or other clinical setting. The mental health professional assesses the individual's mental state and determines if they meet the criteria for involuntary commitment.

3. Court Involvement: In many jurisdictions, a court hearing is required to approve involuntary commitment. The individual has the right to legal representation and can present their case to the court. The court will consider the evidence presented by mental health professionals and make

a determination regarding the need for involuntary commitment.

4. Duration of Commitment: Involuntary commitment is typically temporary and subject to periodic review. Depending on the jurisdiction and the person's condition, the commitment may be for a few days, weeks, or months.

5. Legal Rights: Individuals who are subject to involuntary commitment retain certain legal rights, including the right to legal counsel, the right to refuse treatment (in some cases), the right to appeal the commitment, and the right to be treated with dignity and respect.

6. Least Restrictive Alternative: In many jurisdictions, involuntary commitment must be the least restrictive alternative available. This means that efforts must be made to provide appropriate treatment and care in the least restrictive environment possible.

7. Psychiatric Advance Directives: Some jurisdictions allow individuals to create psychiatric advance directives, which are legal documents that outline their preferences for mental health treatment in the event of a crisis. These directives can help guide decisions about treatment and commitment.

Involuntary commitment is a serious and complex legal process that should only be used as a last resort when the safety of the individual or others is at risk. It is important to balance the need to protect individuals with mental health conditions with respect for their autonomy and rights. Legal professionals, mental health providers, and family members all play crucial roles in ensuring that involuntary commitment is carried out in a fair and compassionate manner, with a focus on providing appropriate care and support to those in need.

Mental health and child custody evaluations

Mental health and child custody evaluations are conducted to assess the mental and emotional well-being of parents or caregivers involved in a custody dispute. These evaluations aim to determine what custody arrangement would be in the best interests of the child based on the mental health of the parents and how it might impact the child's safety, stability, and overall well-being.

Here are some key aspects of mental health and child custody evaluations:

1. Purpose: The primary purpose of these evaluations is to provide the court with an unbiased and professional assessment of the mental health of the parents or caregivers involved in the custody dispute. The evaluation helps the court make informed decisions about custody and visitation arrangements.
2. Evaluation Process: Mental health and child custody evaluations are typically conducted by mental health professionals, such as psychologists or psychiatrists, who have specialized training in family law and child custody matters. The evaluator gathers information through interviews, psychological testing, and reviews of relevant documents.
3. Parental Mental Health: The evaluator assesses the mental health of each parent, looking for any signs of mental health conditions, emotional stability, coping skills, and the ability to provide a safe and nurturing environment for the child.
4. Parent-Child Relationship: The evaluator also

examines the relationship between each parent and the child, looking for signs of attachment, emotional connection, and the ability of the parent to meet the child's emotional needs.

5. Substance Abuse and Other Issues: In addition to mental health, the evaluator may also assess other issues that could impact the child's well-being, such as substance abuse, domestic violence history, or any other relevant factors.

6. Recommendations: Based on the evaluation, the mental health professional provides the court with recommendations regarding custody and visitation arrangements that are in the best interests of the child.

7. Expert Testimony: In some cases, the evaluator may be called to testify in court about their findings and recommendations.

It is essential to ensure that mental health and child custody evaluations are conducted by qualified and experienced professionals to maintain the integrity and validity of the process. The goal is to protect the well-being of the child while taking into account the mental health needs of the parents or caregivers involved in the custody dispute. These evaluations can be valuable tools in helping the court make decisions that prioritize the child's best interests in complex custody cases.

Family Law and Inheritance

Family law and inheritance are closely interconnected when it comes to distributing assets and property after a person's death. Inheritance laws vary significantly from one jurisdiction to another, and they can be influenced by cultural, religious, and legal factors. Here are some key aspects of family law and inheritance:

1. Intestate Succession: When a person dies without a valid will, their estate is distributed according to the laws of intestate succession. These laws determine how the deceased person's assets and property are divided among their surviving family members, such as spouses, children, parents, and siblings.

2. Wills and Testaments: A will is a legal document that allows a person (the testator) to specify how they want their assets and property to be distributed after their death. It can also include provisions for the care of minor children and the appointment of guardians. Having a valid will ensures that the testator's wishes are carried out and can help prevent disputes among family members.

3. Probate: Probate is the legal process of validating a will and distributing the deceased person's estate according to its terms. The court oversees this process, and an executor or personal representative is usually appointed to administer the estate.

4. Community Property vs. Common Law Property: In some jurisdictions, assets acquired during a marriage are considered community property and are equally

owned by both spouses. In contrast, common law property systems treat assets acquired during a marriage as individually owned, unless specified otherwise.

5. Inheritance Tax: Some jurisdictions impose an inheritance tax or estate tax on the assets and property inherited by beneficiaries. The tax rates and exemptions can vary depending on the jurisdiction.

6. Family Provision Laws: In certain jurisdictions, family provision laws allow certain family members or dependents to claim a share of the deceased person's estate, even if they were not adequately provided for in the will.

7. Blended Families: In cases of blended families, where one or both spouses have children from previous relationships, estate planning can become more complex. Wills and other legal documents should be carefully crafted to address the needs and interests of all family members.

8. Trusts and Estate Planning: Some individuals use trusts as part of their estate planning to manage and distribute assets in a way that provides for their family's needs while minimizing tax liabilities.

It is crucial for individuals to seek legal advice from a qualified attorney to ensure their estate planning aligns with their wishes and to navigate the complexities of family law and inheritance laws. By carefully planning and understanding their options, individuals can help safeguard their assets and ensure that their loved ones are provided for after their passing.

Intestate succession and wills

Intestate succession and wills are two fundamental concepts in family law and inheritance that dictate how a person's assets and property are distributed after their death. Let's explore each of them in more detail:

1. Intestate Succession: Intestate succession refers to the legal process of distributing a deceased person's assets and property when they die without a valid will or without specifying certain assets in their will. In such cases, the distribution is governed by the laws of the state or country where the deceased person resided at the time of their death.

The laws of intestate succession typically prioritize the deceased person's closest living relatives, such as their spouse, children, parents, and siblings, in determining who inherits their assets. The distribution is often based on a predetermined order of priority, and the share each heir receives depends on the jurisdiction's laws and the specific family situation.

It is essential to note that intestate succession laws can vary significantly between jurisdictions, so the distribution of assets may differ based on where the deceased person lived at the time of their death. In some cases, distant relatives or even the state may inherit the deceased person's assets if there are no surviving close relatives.

2. Wills: A will is a legal document that allows a person (the testator) to specify how they want their assets and property to be distributed after their death. In a

will, the testator can name beneficiaries and allocate specific assets or properties to each beneficiary. They can also appoint an executor to carry out their wishes and handle the administrative tasks related to the distribution of their estate.

Wills are essential tools for individuals to ensure that their assets are distributed according to their wishes. It allows the testator to provide for their loved ones, appoint guardians for minor children, leave bequests to charitable organizations, and even establish trusts for specific purposes.

By having a valid will, the testator can avoid the laws of intestate succession, which might distribute their assets differently from what they intended. Wills also provide an opportunity for the testator to reduce potential family conflicts and ensure that their loved ones are taken care of after their passing.

It is advisable for individuals to consult with an attorney experienced in estate planning and family law to create a well-drafted and legally valid will. Regular updates to the will may be necessary to reflect any changes in family circumstances, assets, or preferences.

In summary, intestate succession governs the distribution of assets when a person dies without a will, while a will allows individuals to control the distribution of their assets and ensure that their wishes are carried out after their death. Both concepts are crucial in family law and inheritance planning to protect the interests of the deceased person and their loved ones.

Inheritance rights of surviving spouses and children

Inheritance rights of surviving spouses and children are essential aspects of family law and estate planning. These rights vary depending on the jurisdiction and applicable laws, but some common principles are observed in many places:

1. Inheritance Rights of Surviving Spouses: In most jurisdictions, surviving spouses have certain inheritance rights even if the deceased spouse did not leave a will. These rights are often referred to as "spousal rights of election" or "spousal share."

These rights typically entitle the surviving spouse to a portion of the deceased spouse's estate, regardless of what the deceased spouse's will states. The exact share may vary depending on the jurisdiction's laws and the length of the marriage. In some cases, the surviving spouse may be entitled to half or a specific percentage of the estate.

2. Inheritance Rights of Children: Children also have inheritance rights in the estate of their deceased parents, even if the parents died without a will. The laws of intestate succession typically provide for the distribution of the deceased person's estate among their surviving children.

The distribution may be divided equally among all the children, or it may take into account specific circumstances, such as the presence of adopted or stepchildren. In cases where there is a surviving spouse and children, the laws may allocate a portion of the estate to the spouse and the remaining balance to the children.

3. Right to Contest a Will: In some situations, surviving spouses and children have the right to contest a will if they believe that it is invalid or that it does not adequately provide for their needs. This is especially relevant if the will disinherits the surviving spouse or children or if they suspect that the deceased was unduly influenced or lacked mental capacity when creating the will.

Contesting a will can be a complex legal process, and it is advisable for individuals with concerns about a will to seek legal counsel.

It is important to note that inheritance laws can be intricate and may vary significantly between jurisdictions. Consulting with an experienced estate planning attorney is crucial for individuals to understand their specific inheritance rights and take appropriate steps to protect their interests. Proper estate planning, including the creation of a will, can help ensure that the wishes of the deceased are fulfilled and that surviving spouses and children are appropriately provided for after their passing.

Estate planning and family law considerations

Estate planning and family law are closely intertwined, as the decisions made during the estate planning process can have significant implications for family members and loved ones. Here are some key considerations where estate planning and family law intersect:

1. Wills and Trusts: Creating a comprehensive will or trust is a vital aspect of estate planning. A will allows individuals to specify how they want their assets distributed after their death, including property, finances, and personal belongings. Trusts, on the other hand, can provide more control over asset distribution and may offer benefits like avoiding probate or reducing estate taxes.

2. Guardianship Designations: Parents with minor children should include guardianship designations in their estate plans. This ensures that if something happens to both parents, a trusted individual or family member is legally appointed to care for and make decisions on behalf of the children.

3. Marital Agreements: Marital agreements, such as prenuptial agreements or postnuptial agreements, can address financial matters and property rights within the context of family law and estate planning. These agreements can protect assets and specify how property will be distributed in the event of divorce or death.

4. Beneficiary Designations: Reviewing and updating beneficiary designations on retirement accounts, life insurance policies, and other assets is crucial to ensure that the intended individuals receive those assets upon the account holder's death. Beneficiary designations typically override the instructions in a will, so it is essential to keep them up to date.

5. Health Care Directives: Health care directives, including living wills and medical powers of attorney, allow individuals to express their medical treatment preferences and appoint someone they trust to make medical decisions on their behalf if they become incapacitated.

6. Consideration of Special Family Circumstances: Estate planning should take into account any special family circumstances, such as blended families, children from previous marriages, or individuals with special needs. These situations may require specific provisions to ensure all family members are provided for appropriately.

7. Business Succession Planning: Family-owned businesses may require specific succession planning to ensure a smooth transfer of ownership and management to the next generation.

8. Long-Term Care Planning: Estate planning can also involve considerations for long-term care, such as setting up trusts to protect assets or exploring insurance options to cover potential long-term care expenses.

Estate planning and family law are complex areas that require careful thought and consideration. It is advisable for individuals and families to work with experienced estate planning attorneys who can tailor plans to their unique circumstances and goals. Regular review and updates to estate plans are also essential to ensure they remain relevant and effective as life circumstances change.

Future Trends and Challenges in Family Law

Family law continues to evolve to meet the changing needs and dynamics of modern families. Several future trends and challenges are likely to shape the field of family law:

1. Technology and Digital Assets: As technology advances, issues related to digital assets, online accounts, and social media profiles will become more prevalent in family law. Addressing the division of digital assets and privacy concerns will require updated legal frameworks.

2. Non-Traditional Family Structures: The definition of family continues to expand beyond traditional nuclear families. Same-sex couples, unmarried partners, and non-biological parents are becoming more common. Family law will need to adapt to accommodate the legal rights and responsibilities of these diverse family structures.

3. Surrogacy and Assisted Reproduction: Advancements in reproductive technologies raise complex legal questions related to surrogacy agreements, parental rights, and custody disputes involving children born through assisted reproduction methods.

4. Co-Parenting and Shared Custody: The focus on children's best interests has led to an increased emphasis on shared custody arrangements and co-parenting after divorce or separation. Future family law may explore more innovative ways to support

effective co-parenting relationships.

5. International Family Law: With the growing mobility of families across borders, international family law will face challenges related to jurisdiction, child abduction, and the recognition of foreign family law judgments.

6. Elder Law: As the global population ages, family law will address issues related to elder abuse, guardianship, and long-term care planning for older adults.

7. Mental Health and Family Law: Family law professionals may increasingly collaborate with mental health experts to address mental health concerns that impact child custody and parenting arrangements.

8. Alternative Dispute Resolution: Mediation, collaborative law, and other alternative dispute resolution methods are gaining popularity for resolving family law matters. Emphasizing collaborative approaches can lead to more positive outcomes and reduce adversarial litigation.

9. Cultural Sensitivity: Family law must be sensitive to diverse cultural practices and traditions, ensuring that legal processes respect the cultural values and beliefs of families from different backgrounds.

10. Access to Justice: Improving access to justice for all individuals, regardless of their financial situation, will remain an ongoing challenge in family law. Expanding legal aid and resources for low-income families will be essential.

Family law practitioners will need to stay informed about emerging legal trends and be prepared to navigate complex legal issues with empathy and professionalism. Collaborating with other professionals, including mental health experts and financial planners, can provide comprehensive support for

families during challenging times.

Evolving family structures and legal implications

As society continues to change and evolve, family structures have become increasingly diverse. Some of the evolving family structures include:

1. Same-Sex Couples: The recognition of same-sex marriage and legal rights for LGBTQ+ couples has brought significant changes to family law. Same-sex couples now have the same legal rights and responsibilities as opposite-sex couples when it comes to marriage, divorce, adoption, and child custody.

2. Blended Families: Blended families, where one or both partners have children from previous relationships, present unique legal challenges. Family law addresses issues such as step-parent adoption, child custody arrangements, and financial support for children from previous marriages.

3. Cohabiting Couples: Many couples choose to cohabit without getting married. In some jurisdictions, there are legal implications for unmarried couples in terms of property rights, financial support, and child custody.

4. Single-Parent Families: The number of single-parent families has been on the rise. Family law plays a crucial role in determining child custody, visitation rights, and child support for single parents.

5. Childless Couples: Some couples choose not to have children. Family law may come into play in areas such

as estate planning and inheritance rights.

6. Grandparent and Extended Family Roles: In some cases, grandparents or other extended family members may seek legal rights, such as visitation or custody, when it is in the best interests of the child.

7. Non-Biological Parental Rights: Family law has evolved to recognize the legal rights of non-biological parents, such as those who have assumed a parental role through adoption or long-term care.

8. Solo Parenting and Assisted Reproduction: With advancements in assisted reproduction technologies, solo parenting is becoming more common. Family law addresses issues related to parental rights, child support, and custody in these cases.

The legal implications of evolving family structures vary by jurisdiction and can be complex. Family law continues to adapt to meet the needs of diverse families and ensure that all individuals are treated fairly and equitably. It is essential for legal professionals to stay informed about these changes and be sensitive to the unique circumstances of each family they serve.

Technological advancements and family law

Technological advancements have significantly impacted family law in various ways, streamlining processes and introducing new challenges. Some key technological advancements in family law include:

1. Electronic Filing and Case Management: Many family courts have implemented electronic filing systems and case management software. This has improved the efficiency of document processing, case tracking, and communication between parties and their attorneys.

2. Online Dispute Resolution (ODR): ODR platforms have emerged as a means of resolving family law disputes online. This can include virtual mediation, negotiation, and arbitration, providing a convenient and cost-effective alternative to traditional court proceedings.

3. Virtual Court Hearings: With the advent of video conferencing technology, virtual court hearings have become more common. This has facilitated remote participation for parties and witnesses, reducing the need for physical court appearances and easing the burden on families.

4. Communication and Co-Parenting Apps: Various apps and software have been developed to facilitate communication and co-parenting between divorced or separated parents. These tools allow for shared calendars, messaging, and document sharing related to child custody arrangements and visitation schedules.

5. Digital Evidence and Social Media: Family law cases increasingly involve digital evidence, such as social media posts, emails, and text messages. These can play a crucial role in matters such as child custody, divorce, and spousal support disputes.

6. Artificial Intelligence (AI) in Legal Research: AI-powered legal research tools have revolutionized how attorneys access and analyze legal information. This has led to more accurate and efficient legal advice and representation in family law cases.

7. Blockchain Technology and Smart Contracts: Blockchain technology has the potential to revolutionize aspects of family law, such as prenuptial agreements and property division. Smart contracts can automate the enforcement of certain family law provisions.

8. Privacy and Security Concerns: As family law increasingly involves the use of digital technology and online platforms, privacy and security concerns have become more significant. Safeguarding sensitive information is critical to protect the interests of the parties involved.

9. Online Family Mediation: Virtual family mediation services have become more prevalent, allowing parties to engage in mediation remotely and in a comfortable environment, promoting more effective communication and resolution of disputes.

10. Data Analytics and Predictive Modeling: Data analytics and predictive modeling can help attorneys assess the potential outcomes of family law cases based on historical data, leading to more informed decision-making.

While technology has brought numerous benefits to family law, it also presents challenges in terms of data privacy, digital evidence authentication, and ensuring equitable access to technology. Legal professionals and policymakers need to remain attuned to these advancements to address the evolving needs and concerns of families in the digital age.

Balancing cultural diversity and legal uniformity

Balancing cultural diversity and legal uniformity is an important consideration in family law. Family law operates within a complex societal framework where diverse cultural practices, beliefs, and norms shape family dynamics and relationships. At the same time, legal systems seek to establish consistent and predictable rules that apply uniformly to all individuals, regardless of their cultural background.

Key considerations for striking this balance include:

1. Cultural Sensitivity: Family law professionals must be culturally sensitive and aware of the diverse beliefs and practices of the communities they serve. Understanding cultural differences can help ensure that legal proceedings are conducted in a respectful and inclusive manner.

2. Customary Practices: Some communities may have customary practices that differ from mainstream legal norms. Where appropriate, family law may recognize and accommodate these practices to preserve cultural identity and maintain community cohesion.

3. Legal Pluralism: In certain jurisdictions, legal pluralism may exist, allowing for the coexistence of formal legal systems and customary or religious legal systems. Courts may recognize certain aspects of customary law while still upholding fundamental legal principles.

4. Children's Rights: While respecting cultural diversity, family law must prioritize the best interests of children. Universal children's rights, as outlined in international treaties, serve as a guiding framework to protect children's welfare irrespective of cultural backgrounds.

5. Human Rights and Equality: Family law must uphold fundamental human rights principles, ensuring that individuals are treated equally before the law regardless of their cultural background.

6. Mediation and Alternative Dispute Resolution: Mediation and other alternative dispute resolution methods can provide flexible approaches to resolving family law issues, allowing parties to incorporate culturally sensitive solutions.

7. Education and Training: Legal professionals should undergo cultural competency training to better understand and navigate the complexities of cultural diversity in family law cases.

8. Community Engagement: Engaging with communities and community leaders can help build understanding and trust between the legal system and diverse cultural groups.

9. Legal Framework Flexibility: Family law frameworks should be designed with flexibility to accommodate cultural diversity while preserving core legal principles.

10. Legislative Review: Periodic review of family law statutes ensures that they remain relevant and responsive to the evolving cultural dynamics within society.

Balancing cultural diversity and legal uniformity is a dynamic process that requires ongoing dialogue and cooperation between legal professionals, policymakers, and cultural communities. By valuing cultural diversity while maintaining legal uniformity, family law can better serve the diverse needs of families in today's multicultural societies.

Recapitulation of key insights and themes discussed in the book

"Family Law: Foundations and Modern Dynamics" delves into the multifaceted world of family law, examining its historical roots, legal principles, and evolving challenges. Throughout the book, several key insights and themes are explored:

1. Family Law's Purpose: Family law is an essential branch of legal practice that governs the intricate relationships and dynamics within families. Its primary focus is to protect the interests and rights of family members and promote stable and equitable family structures.

2. Evolving Family Structures: The book recognizes the diversity of family structures in modern society, including same-sex couples, blended families, and single-parent households. Family law has adapted to accommodate these changes, ensuring that all family members are afforded legal protection and recognition.

3. Children's Best Interests: A recurring theme is the paramount consideration of children's best interests in family law matters. Courts and legal professionals strive to make decisions that promote the well-being and welfare of children involved in divorce, custody, and adoption cases.

4. Legal Processes and Alternatives: The book emphasizes the importance of alternative dispute resolution methods, such as mediation and collaborative law,

in resolving family law disputes. These approaches encourage open communication and cooperation, reducing the emotional toll on families.

5. Intersectionality and Diversity: Family law intersects with various areas of law and addresses a wide range of issues, including domestic violence, mental health, elder care, and reproductive technologies. The book highlights the significance of recognizing and addressing the diverse needs of families from different cultural, socioeconomic, and ethnic backgrounds.

6. International Aspects: Family law extends beyond national borders, and the book examines the complexities of international family law cases, such as child abduction and recognition of foreign marriages.

7. Balancing Tradition and Modernity: Family law grapples with the tension between traditional values and evolving societal norms. The book explores how legal systems must strike a balance between preserving cultural heritage and safeguarding individual rights and equality.

8. Legal Protections and Vulnerable Populations: Family law plays a critical role in protecting vulnerable populations, such as victims of domestic violence and children in need of care and protection. It addresses the challenges faced by these individuals and aims to provide effective legal remedies.

9. Ethical Considerations: Throughout the book, ethical considerations in family law practice are underscored, particularly when dealing with sensitive and emotionally charged cases. Legal professionals are encouraged to approach their work with empathy, compassion, and a commitment to upholding justice.

10. Adapting to Change: The book acknowledges the dynamic nature of family law, requiring continuous adaptation to reflect societal shifts, technological advancements, and emerging

family dynamics.

Overall, "Family Law: Foundations and Modern Dynamics" presents a comprehensive exploration of the complexities, challenges, and essential principles governing family law. It encourages readers to approach family law matters with an open mind, a dedication to justice, and a focus on promoting the well-being of families and individuals alike.

The importance of family law in shaping relationships and society's well-being

Family law plays a crucial role in shaping relationships and society's well-being in several significant ways:

1. Preserving Family Structure: Family law provides the legal framework for establishing and preserving family structures, such as marriage, domestic partnerships, and adoption. By defining these relationships, family law contributes to the stability and coherence of families, which are the fundamental building blocks of society.

2. Protecting Children's Rights: Family law prioritizes the best interests of children, ensuring their rights and well-being are safeguarded. It addresses matters of child custody, visitation, and support, striving to create nurturing environments for children in both intact and separated families.

3. Promoting Fair Division of Assets: In divorce or dissolution of marriage cases, family law addresses the equitable division of assets and property. This ensures that both parties are treated fairly and allows them to move forward with their lives after the end of their marriage.

4. Supporting Vulnerable Populations: Family law plays a crucial role in protecting vulnerable populations, including victims of domestic violence, elderly individuals, and children in need of care and protection. Legal mechanisms, such as

restraining orders and guardianship arrangements, provide crucial support to those facing challenging circumstances.

5. Encouraging Alternative Dispute Resolution: Family law encourages the use of alternative dispute resolution methods like mediation and collaborative law. These approaches promote open communication, cooperation, and resolution outside of court, reducing the emotional strain on families and facilitating amicable outcomes.

6. Addressing Reproductive Technologies: As reproductive technologies advance, family law addresses legal issues related to surrogacy, egg and sperm donation, and parentage. This ensures that legal parentage is established, protecting the rights and responsibilities of all parties involved.

7. Fostering Social Cohesion: Family law plays a significant role in fostering social cohesion and maintaining societal values. By recognizing diverse family structures, including same-sex couples and blended families, family law promotes inclusivity and diversity within society.

8. Ensuring Justice and Fairness: Family law is rooted in principles of justice, fairness, and equality. It provides a framework for resolving disputes and conflicts in a manner that upholds individual rights while considering the needs of the family unit.

9. Recognizing Interconnectedness: Family law recognizes the interconnectedness of family members and the impact of individual decisions on the broader family unit. It takes into account the emotional and financial ties between family members, emphasizing the importance of maintaining these bonds.

10. Promoting Social Stability: A robust family law system contributes to social stability by providing clear legal guidelines and procedures for addressing

family matters. When families have access to legal protections and remedies, it reduces the potential for conflict and instability within society.

Overall, family law is integral to shaping relationships and promoting society's well-being. It provides a legal framework that supports the rights and needs of individuals within families, fosters inclusivity and fairness, and contributes to the overall social fabric of communities. By addressing the complexities of family dynamics and offering legal solutions, family law plays a crucial role in the functioning and cohesiveness of societies worldwide.